Either Jew or Gentile

EITHER JEW OR GENTILE

Paul's Unfolding Theology of Inclusivity

Eung Chun Park

Westminster John Knox Press
LOUISVILLE • LONDON

© 2003 Eung Chun Park

Book design by Sharon Adams
Cover design © 2003 Eric Handel, LMNOP

First edition
Published by Westminster John Knox Press
Louisville, Kentucky

This book is printed on acid-free paper that meets the American National Standards Institute Z39.48 standard. ∞

PRINTED IN THE UNITED STATES OF AMERICA

03 04 05 06 07 08 09 10 11 12 — 10 9 8 7 6 5 4 3 2 1

Library of Congress Cataloging-in-Publication Data
Park, Eung Chun, 1958–
    Either Jew or Gentile : Paul's unfolding theology of inclusivity /
Eung Chun Park.—1st ed.
      p. cm.
    Includes bibliographical references and indexes.
    ISBN 0-664-22453-9 (alk. paper)
      1. Paul, the Apostle, Saint.   2. Bible. N.T. Epistles of Paul—Theology.
3. Gentiles in the New Testament.   4. Church history—Primitive and early church,
ca. 30–600.   I. Title.

BS2506.3 .P37 2003
225.9'2—dc21   2002038090

To my wife
Younghee Kim Park

Contents

Preface

This book is about the life of Paul, the "apostle" of Christ to the Gentiles. It is not a comprehensive biography of Paul but a focused retelling of the story of a particular segment of his life, that is, the struggle to include "others" in the fold of God's people. The issue of whether to engage in Gentile mission and, for those who were favorably disposed to endorse it, the question of how to receive the Gentiles caused a serious tension in earliest Christianity during the mid-first century C.E., while it still remained a Jewish phenomenon. The result of this tension set the trajectories of universalism and particularism for the subsequent history of early Christianity.

This book surveys the history of conflict in some early Christian communities over the terms of receiving the Gentiles. It will show how the two gospels, the gospel of the circumcision and the gospel of the uncircumcision, did and did not get along with each other at different times and in different occasions in the pristine period of early Christian mission, and it will show how Paul dealt with the clash between the two in both practical and theological terms. My primary goal in writing this book is to provide a coherent narrative of Paul's struggle to defend his gospel, of which the quintessential principle is to accept "others"—in this case, Gentiles—as they are.

In the course of this long struggle there is a fascinating development in Paul's thought that he makes heuristically. It is my conviction that both the *story* of his struggle and the *theological development* that accompanies it have a profound message for contemporary Christians who face the challenge of redefining our identity vis-à-vis "others" in this increasingly pluralistic, postmodern, global village. In that context, what I ultimately hope for is to facilitate and invite further discussion on the nature and contours of Paul's struggle to include Gentiles without forcing them to be who they are not. I believe the story of Paul told in this book has many rich ramifications for our understanding of the history of earliest

Christianity as well as for our constructive theology of "others," which will definitely have an impact on Christian ecclesiology, soteriology, and missiology.

My fascination with Paul began with Professor Hans Dieter Betz's seminar on 2 Corinthians at the University of Chicago, which introduced me to the intriguing dynamics of the relation between literature and history behind the complex fragmentary hypotheses of this otherwise incomprehensible text. It was as if some puzzle pieces were gradually put together for the whole picture to emerge. Also, the inclusion of the Gentiles in early Christian communities has long been an area of interest for me. It was an important subject in the first century C.E. and it has become an even more important one in the twenty-first century C.E. because of its immediate relevance to the similar issues in our time.

The main ideas for this book have been formed over the years of teaching various courses on Paul at San Francisco Theological Seminary and at the Graduate Theological Union since 1996, but the substantial portion of the actual writing was done in 1999, while I was staying at the University of Cambridge, England, for my sabbatical research. The University Faculty of Divinity, Westminster College, and Tyndale Library provided me with superb research resources, not to mention the great opportunities of interacting with various scholars I had the privilege to meet at this richly international scholarly community. So, I am profoundly grateful first to the faculty and the board of San Francisco Theological Seminary for granting me such a generous sabbatical leave and then to all the Cambridge people who made my stay there fruitful and extremely enjoyable.

Lewis R. Rambo, a specialist on religious conversion, and Alan F. Segal, an expert on Second Temple and Early Rabbinic Judaism, read the earlier version of the chapter on "Particularism and Universalism in Mediterranean Antiquity" and gave me helpful feedback. Needless to say, however, I am solely responsible for whatever remaining shortcomings there are. Davis Perkins, president of Presbyterian Publishing Corporation, took a keen interest in this project when it was still in an amorphous stage and initiated the daunting "formal" process of publication for me. Carey Newman, then acquisition editor at Westminster John Knox Press, carried it through various stages of the decision-making process and also helped me set the tone of the book and deal with the art of laying out its content. After Newman's departure from WJK, Janice Catron, the editorial director, continued to provide me with excellent editorial support. Without the assistance of these people this book would not have seen the light of publication. I am immensely thankful to them all.

Eung Chun Park

San Francisco Theological Seminary

Introduction

One of the characteristics of the postmodern ethos is its openness to diversity. Postmodernity fosters willingness as well as ability to recognize authenticity in all kinds of "other"-ness. One of its practical implications is an inclusive way of being and thinking both in academia and in society in general, which takes a number of different forms such as multiculturalism or religious pluralism. Whether one embraces pluralism or not, it is no longer possible for anybody to ignore the issue, and having to deal with such an issue engenders the need to reconsider many of the conventional terms of defining one's self-identity as well as one's view on "others." This is true for religion, especially in the Judeo-Christian-Islamic tradition, which holds a very strong monotheistic belief.[1]

Christianity has been universalistic and at the same time very particularistic in terms of its dealings with others. Its belief in the universal applicability of the salvific redemption of Jesus Christ gave it an almost unprecedented urge to world mission, but precisely because of the same belief it has tended to develop a highly exclusive soteriology, which often became a pretext for religious, cultural, and political imperialism. This would not have been felt as a serious problem in the era of "Christendom." Since we now live in a pluralistic, postmodern, and post-Christendom society, however, the time is ripe for Christianity to look back on its nascent history of mission from the perspective of the tension between universalism and particularism in order to reassess how this tension impacted the nature of Christian sensibility concerning inclusivity and exclusivity. Such a hermeneutically oriented historical study will contribute not only to a better understanding of the past but also to a clearer direction for the future of Christianity.

This book is a reconstruction of the history of the tension between particularism and universalism in earliest Christianity, focusing on the struggle of

Paul to defend the validity of the Torah-free *gospel of the uncircumcision* (τὸ εὐαγγέλιον τῆς ἀκροβυστίας, Gal. 2:7) vis-à-vis the Torah-bound *gospel of the circumcision* ([τὸ εὐαγγέλιον] τῆς περιτομῆς, Gal. 2:7) of his opponents, who asserted their representation of the authority of the Jerusalem church. By using such terms as "Torah-bound gospel" and "Torah-free gospel," I have no intention to imply one is better than the other. They are just two different ways of trying to be faithful to the will of God. Both presuppose the grace of God as the foundation of salvation. They are different in understanding how the grace is dispensed to humans. In that regard, it is important *not* to confuse the distinction between the gospel of the circumcision and the gospel of the uncircumcision with that between Judaism and Christianity. Theologically as well as historically, both the gospels were still within the purview of Judaism. Not even the "Torah-free" gospel was non-Jewish, let alone anti-Jewish. Paul was not a champion of "Christianity against Judaism." The dichotomy between Judaism and Christianity should not be anachronistically imposed on this distinction between the two gospels in earliest Christianity.

The main body of this book traces the course of the five major events in Paul's career as an "apostle" to the Gentiles, i.e., the Apostolic Council in Jerusalem, the Antioch incident, the Galatian incident, the Corinthian incident, and his last visit to Jerusalem. The survey of these landmark events will show how the issue of the two gospels played itself out in Paul's life and how it impacted his theology. With this historical reconstruction I will demonstrate that *Paul's theology changed as he went through these tumultuous experiences*, confirming the premise that his theology was always a "work in progress" and that it grew out of the concrete historical and existential realities that he found himself in. It is my conviction that the horizon of Paul's soteriology was substantially broadened in the last phase of his life and theology,[2] and that he came to accept *both* the "Torah-bound gospel" *and* the "Torah-free gospel" as ways that proclaim Christ. To this extent, Paul's developing theology of inclusivity led him eventually to concede that either gospel fits within the greater scope of mission. This aspect has been largely neglected or least appreciated in New Testament scholarship, and I hope this book will make a small contribution to a new understanding on this subject.

The issue of the salvation of Gentiles was no trivial matter in early Christianity, and the New Testament bears witness to a substantial disagreement among different early Christian communities concerning their understanding of how Gentiles should be incorporated into the church. This disagreement caused severe conflicts within early Christian communities, especially in Paul's churches, with the result that the question of Gentile mission and its ramifications for soteriology became one of the most important theological issues in the first chapter of the history of early Christianity.

The question concerning "Gentiles" is obviously a Jewish one, and as such it has much to do with the historic tension between particularism and universalism, which existed in Judaism long before Christianity was born. It was still a current issue in Judaism in the first century C.E. The issue became even sharper after

70 C.E., when Jewish people had to redefine their religious identity without the temple, which had long been their central symbol. It is in this environment that early Christianity emerged initially as a Jewish phenomenon and therefore it naturally inherited the theological question concerning the Gentiles from its mother religion.

However, some words of caution are in order here. First, such technical terms as particularism and universalism are often used by different people for different meanings, and like most technical terms they defy fixed definition. Mindful of this, I will try to provide in the following section working definitions of these terms as I use them in this book. Second, I am painfully aware of the naïveté of the once-traditional Christian notion that Judaism represented particularism whereas Christianity embodied universalism. This kind of "superiority complex" of Christian triumphalism, which plagued the minds of many Christian theologians throughout history, is absolutely an ill-conceived perception. The reality is that particularism and universalism coexist in most institutions, religious or otherwise. Neither Judaism nor Christianity was an exception. In that vein, one could say the early Christian tension between particularism and universalism mirrored the same tension that existed in Judaism.

In this book I will attempt to reconstruct the major course of events in the life of Paul and his communities from the historical data embedded in various corpora of literature in the New Testament and other related documents. Therefore, the primary method of approach will be historical investigation based on critical interpretation of pertinent literature. As is the case with any ancient history, reconstruction of the history of mission in early Christianity suffers from lack of sufficient data. Oftentimes what we have available is only indirect allusions or cryptic references, which means we sometimes have to rely on an informed conjecture in order to supply the missing links and to construct a coherent narrative. The end result would be a hypothetical reconstruction of the history of mission that best accounts for the currently available data.

In terms of the data for historical reconstruction of the conflict regarding Gentile mission in Pauline communities, I will primarily concentrate on the undisputed epistles of Paul—especially Galatians, 1–2 Corinthians, Romans, and Philippians. The use of Acts is extremely difficult in this case, because the author of Acts has a theological agenda to present an idealistic picture of the pristine period of early Christianity. This gives him a definite redactional tendency to gloss over conflicts or tensions, which is the very topic of this book. So I will use passages from Acts with caution and only as far as they cohere with Pauline materials. In that context, the issue of the adequacy of using Acts in reconstructing Paul's life will be discussed.

Selections from other sources—notably the synoptic materials, some of the New Testament apocryphal literature, and second-century anti-Pauline polemical documents from Jewish Christianity—will be used to trace the aftermath of the debates concerning the universalistic mission in post-Pauline Christianity in the late first and the second century C.E. Here, universalism as an overarching theme of Luke–Acts will be put in perspective as a legacy of Pauline missiology. Then the Gospel of Matthew will be investigated from the perspective of the final redactor as a Jewish Christian proponent of universalism, who concurs with Paul with respect to missiology but differs from him in soteriology. These pictures from Paul, Luke–Acts, and Matthew will project a coherent picture of an emerging ecumenical Christian church that had its own version of universalism in the second century C.E.

HERMENEUTICAL ASSUMPTIONS

There are several premises that make up the hermeneutical framework for the reconstruction of the trajectories of particularism and universalism in early Christianity described in this book. First of all, this book starts from the recognition that theology matters in the historical reconstruction of early Christianity. It is true that in ancient societies only a tiny fraction of the population was literate and, therefore, abstract theoretical discussion of any kind was reserved only for intellectual elites; ordinary people were largely untouched by ideas, philosophy, or theology. Because religion was an integral part of ancient societies, however, it is also true that religious ideas—even though they were mostly shaped by the elites—did affect the lives of ordinary people who were not active participants in the ongoing intellectual discourses. This was especially the case with early Christianity, which inherited from Judaism a long tradition of religious literature and hermeneutics. Ordinary early Christians, like most Jews, were familiar with the content of their religious literature at least through listening, if not through reading. In other words, the people were orally literate and therefore they were not totally unequipped for theological thinking. Indeed, it is to the ordinary members of his churches that Paul addressed his epistles, which were loaded with theological ideas.

Therefore, this book is based on the premise that theology played an important role in the life of the earliest Christian communities—and in the course of the history of earliest Christianity. No one would dispute that theology was a crucial factor in the christologically centered orthodoxy-and-heresy controversy in the second century C.E. and thereafter, but few seem to take seriously that theology mattered in the first century C.E. as well. This book argues that for earliest Christianity in the mid-first century C.E. the most important theological issue was soteriology defined in missiological terms: that is, the question of how Gentiles qua Gentiles should or should not be included in the people of God. Furthermore, this book maintains that, because the earliest Christian communities were Jewish, they existed and interacted with one another in the intramural tension between particularism and universalism that *already* existed in Judaism.

Second, this book is written from the perspective that the trajectories of early Christianity were shaped not only by opposition from without but also by internal schisms and conflicts. New Testament writings in the mid-first century, largely the Pauline epistles as well as some of the earlier redactional layers of the synoptic traditions, reflect conflicts within early Christianity rather than opposition from outside. This book focuses on the conflict between two opposing theological tendencies in early Christianity and tries to show how that shaped the course of early Christianity in the next phase of its development.

By saying this I am not arguing that conflict is the single most important factor in reconstructing early Christian history. It goes without saying that what made the early Christian communities what they were was their common belief in Jesus Christ. This commonality may outweigh the differences among various Christian communities. When we reconstruct the history of an institution or a phenomenon that has multiple subgroups within it, commonality among the subgroups is more important in the history of that institution vis-à-vis other institutions, whereas differences among them are more important in the history of the internal dynamics of the institution. This book focuses on the latter with regard to the reconstruction of the history of early Christianity.

Also, by highlighting the tension between two different soteriologies, I do not mean to imply that there were only two soteriologies in early Christianity. Most probably, the tension between Jerusalem and Paul with regard to soteriology was just a part of the theological diversity in early Christianity. The tension this book deals with, however, has the most data for historical reconstruction because of the dominant position that Paul posthumously occupied later in the history of Christianity.

Third, this book is not just written out of antiquarian curiosity. I recognize the value of a "disinterested" quest for the reconstruction of the past for its own sake, if such a thing were possible. That is not what gave impetus for this book, though. In writing this book, I intend not only to look back but also to look forward. This book deals with an important theological issue in the history of early Christianity and tries to relate it to the problems that are relevant to contemporary Christians, namely the question of inclusivity in the realm of human religiosity. In a way it is a question of redefining the meaning of Christian mission in today's postmodern pluralistic society.

Because of its immediate connection with cultural imperialism, the very notion of universalistic Christian mission has become a point of criticism both from within and from without. The issue of mission is becoming even more controversial as we move past the era of Christendom into a more pluralistic world, which almost by default does not recognize any religion as having a claim to a privileged status as the "universal" religion. The challenge is how Christians can maintain integrity while they affirm their mission to witness to God's grace through Christ to the world and at the same time to genuinely embrace the reality of God's freedom to dispense grace to whomever God wishes and in whatever way God chooses.

Therefore, I think the time is ripe for the theme of mission in the New Testament to be addressed both historically and hermeneutically, as we find ourselves facing the challenge of redefining the meaning of Christian mission in the context of a postmodern pluralistic society. I understand that the task of dealing with the contemporary meaning of mission is primarily the responsibility of missiologists. To the degree that Christian missiology should be based on the Bible and informed by the earliest history of mission, though, my presentation will be able to facilitate dialogue among New Testament scholars, missiologists, and theologians who are interested in interfaith dialogue.

So, even though I will not seek direct answers for contemporary issues from historical investigation, I will try to draw insights from historical traditions for directions for the future. In so doing, I will eventually be advocating a certain theological position which is historically informed and theologically constructed. I hope it will emerge through the course of this book, especially in the last chapter, clearly but in a manner that is suggestive rather than prescriptive.

OUTLINE OF CHAPTERS

The main body of this book is basically a chronologically presented narrative on the subject, framed by a survey of historical background in the beginning and hermeneutical reflections in the end. Chapter 1 puts the theological foundation of early Christian mission in the larger context. It provides a broad sketch of the emergence of universalism in the Hellenic and Hellenistic culture and especially in the religion of Israel. Then I will discuss the two different ways of understanding the relationship between Jews and Gentiles in Judaism as the immediate background for the tension in early Christianity concerning the issues pertaining to Gentile mission.

Chapter 2 deals with the beginning of early Christianity, focusing on the change of leadership at the Jerusalem church and the foundation and mission of the Antioch church. This chapter will show that one of the very few things about the history of earliest Christianity that we can be sure of is that a certain tension existed in the Jerusalem church as early as the mid-40s C.E. I will first trace how the two factions in the Jerusalem church eventually developed into two different wings in early Christianity that represented different attitudes toward Gentiles.[3] Then I will discuss the mission of the Antioch church, the "conversion" of Paul, and the "conversion" of Peter as part of a continuum that serves as a critical turning point in the history of early Christian mission as it is portrayed in Acts.[4]

Chapter 3 deals with the growing tension between two conflicting soteriologies in early Christianity. I will introduce to the readers the outbreak of the conflict in early Christianity over the issue of Gentile mission, which was only the beginning of a long series of struggles between two different understandings of the gospel. I will try to reconstruct the contours of tensions and conflicts between the particularism of the Jerusalem church and the universalism of the Antioch church in the late 40s C.E. Special attention will be paid to the theological meaning of the deliberation of the Apostolic Council in Jerusalem, which sanctioned the legitimacy of two different gospels (Gal. 2:7). This chapter also deals with the aftermath of the Apostolic Council in Jerusalem, focusing on the Antioch Incident, which I believe happened shortly after the Jerusalem Council and was indirectly but very closely related to its decision. The event will be reconstructed from Paul's account in Gal. 2:11–14 and it will be viewed from the perspective of two different interpretations of the meaning of the agreement of the Apostolic Council in Jerusalem.

Chapter 4 deals with the Galatian Incident, which happened during Paul's Corinthian stay. Working primarily with Paul's own accounts in Galatians, I will first trace the history of Paul's ministry in Galatia and his subsequent conflicts with the Judaizing intruders in the Galatian church, who denied his apostleship and opposed his universalistic soteriology. Then I will discuss Paul's response to his opponents in light of the decision made at the Apostolic Council in Jerusalem. Comparison with the Antioch Incident will be made in the same context.

Chapter 5 deals with the Corinthian Incident, which happened to Paul during his Ephesian stay. Using the six-fragment hypothesis for 2 Corinthians, I will first reconstruct the communication history between Paul and the Corinthian church. Also, relying on several critical passages in 2 Corinthians and connecting them with the pertinent passages in Galatians, I will identify Paul's opponents in the Corinthian church and their theological position. Then I will discuss Paul's response to it. The question of similarities and differences among the Antioch Incident, the Galatian Incident, and the Corinthian Incident will be discussed.

The previous chapters will have demonstrated how serious the breach was between the universalistic Pauline Christianity and the Torah-bound Jerusalem church. Chapter 6 will highlight the effort on Paul's part to attempt reconciliation through the collection project for Jerusalem. Based on what Paul says in 2 Corinthians 8–9 and Romans 15, I will give an interpretation of the theological meaning of the resumed collection project and its result. I will also discuss Paul's new vision of inclusivity, which is implied in his theological arguments in Romans 9–11 and in his personal statements in Philippians. In so doing, I will demonstrate that Paul's theology, especially soteriology, changes significantly over the ten or so years between Galatians and Philippians.

Chapter 7 will briefly discuss the aftermath of this long series of conflicts between the two soteriologies. Starting with the death of James the Lord's brother and the subsequent disintegration of the Jerusalem church, I will describe the continued rivalry between the Pauline and Jamesian branches of early Christianity in the post-Pauline and post-Jamesian period. I will also discuss the formation of the "catholic" church, in which the Pauline branch became the main stream, integrating various different early Christian traditions. It will show how Jewish Christianity with the Jamesian legacy was marginalized by the then-dominant Gentile Christianity and how that process eventually paralleled with the separation between Judaism and Christianity.

Finally, the concluding chapter will briefly summarize some of the salient points of the historical investigation in this book and relate them to the current theological issue of inclusivity, especially as it pertains to the question of the Christian view of others in an increasingly pluralistic postmodern society. The purpose of this discussion is not to propose a definitive answer but to invite further interdisciplinary dialogues by suggesting some insights gleaned from the historical investigation pursued from a particular hermeneutical angle in this book.

Chapter 1

Particularism and Universalism in Mediterranean Antiquity

PREAMBLE

Religion is part of the rubric of the larger society and therefore religious ideas are often expressions of the Zeitgeist of the society. Universalism and particularism as religious concepts reflect two different ways of viewing oneself and others, which may apply to a far greater realm than religion. So, in order to understand the theological underpinnings of these terms, one should first know the larger cultural milieu out of which they came into being.

This chapter will survey the origin and the development of the concepts *universalism* and *particularism* in the Hellenic and the Hellenistic world. After providing working definitions of these terms, I will discuss how the Greeks saw themselves and others in the classical age and how their perceptions changed, if they did, in the Hellenistic era. Then, I will trace how the same ideas existed and intersected with each other in Jewish thought into the second century C.E. I hope that this chapter will reveal a fundamental commonality of human conceptions across the ethnic and religious borders, lest any religion or ethnic group should claim to be standing on "higher ground" than others and disparage others on these issues.

WORKING DEFINITIONS OF THE TERMS

The English word *universalism* is derived from the Latin adjective *ūniversus*, which is a composite word from *ūni* (< *ūnus* "one") and *versus* (< *vertĕre* "to turn"). So, the etymological sense of the word *universalism* is the idea of "all things turned into/toward one." As for its special meaning in theology, the *Oxford English Dictionary* defines universalism as a "doctrine of universal salvation or redemption."[1]

9

In that vein, the OED also defines the term "universalist" as one who holds the belief that redemption is extended to the entire human kind and not limited to a part of it.[2] These definitions have somewhat limited application because such concepts as "redemption" and "salvation" are not universal even within the realm of religions. However, if these terms are replaced with such generic expressions as "divine favor" or "ultimate state of being," the OED definitions are well taken. So, put in religious terms, universalism is the belief that the *entire* universe is the realm of the deity/deities and that all the creatures in the world are objects of care and concern of the same.[3] This universalistic religious thought is the impetus of mission.[4]

As a diminutive of *pars, partis* (f. "part," "portion"), the Latin feminine noun *particula, ae* (f.) means "a small portion" or "a small part." So, etymologically speaking, the English noun *particularism* has the connotation of privileging only a small part of the whole. In religion, the term *particularism* generally refers to the idea that a certain group of people monopolizes a special privilege in relation to the deity, which sets them apart from the rest of the human race. The OED defines the theological meaning of particularism as a dogma that divine grace is limited to a selected part of the human race.[5] Even though the term *grace* is typically Judeo-Christian vocabulary, this definition of particularism seems to describe the ethos of the term particularism accurately.

It is interesting to notice that the OED regards exclusiveness as inherent in particularism. This is perhaps true on the surface, but the reality is more complex than that. History tells us that some, if not all, particularists did have a strong missionary zeal, but the ethos of the mission of particularists will be very different from that of universalists. It is important to understand at this point that universalism also has the potential to engender both a highly inclusive attitude toward others and a very exclusive one, depending on how one interprets the notion of the universal validity or applicability of one's ideas in dealing with other people. In other words, if it is true that universalism is the impetus of mission, then there are two kinds of mission, each reflecting a different position on the inclusive-exclusive spectrum: mission that invites and mission that imposes.

The intrinsic ambiguity of the term *universalism* is well articulated by Jon D. Levenson in his discussion of the universal dimension of Jewish particularism:[6]

> Predicated of a religious tradition, the term "universalism" can carry a number of divergent meanings. It may simply refer to the universality of the deity: No other god exists, and the whole world, without exception, is his. Such universalism, however, still allows for pockets of particularism. Although God may be lord of the world, he need not care about the world in its entirety, or he may care about different classes of creatures in different measures. . . . Or, he may single out one set of persons rather than another— such as the people of Israel, the Christian Church, or the Islamic *ummah*— for special favors and special responsibilities.

Thus, the spectrum of universalism and particularism on the one hand and that of inclusivity and exclusivity on the other intersect with one another, rendering all kinds of complex combinations of these four variables that are possible in the human religious arena.

Usually, when a religion with a universalistic outlook attains political/military power, it tends to develop an exclusive theology about otherness and to become imperialistic. Christianity was not immune to this tendency. So, any study on the history of early Christian mission should take into consideration that early Christianity was initially a small minority phenomenon within Judaism itself, let alone in the greater religious landscape of the Mediterranean world in the first century C.E. Early Christianity had no political power with which it could become imperialistic. It is only after Constantine that things changed drastically.

PARTICULARISM AND UNIVERSALISM
IN THE HELLENIC AND THE HELLENISTIC WORLD

Generally speaking, universalism did not exist in the ancient world. In Mediterranean antiquity, religion and culture were largely ethnocentric and particularistic. Greeks usually divided the whole of humanity into two categories: Greeks and barbarians.[7] In *Menexenus*, even though it is not a serious philosophical treatise, the Platonic Socrates recites in a laudatory tone the oration of Aspasia, in which she boastfully says, "We ourselves live [in Athens] as pure Greeks not mixed with barbarians, which is why keen hatred of foreign race has permeated the city [i.e., Athens]."[8] Aristotle cites a line from a poem which says it is natural for Greeks to rule over barbarians, and he further says that barbarians and slaves are the same in nature because the former lack the ability to rule, which is reserved only for the Greeks.[9] The fact that Aristotle quotes a line of poem as if it is well known implies that this kind of idea was rather popular among the Greeks at that time. One may call it "Greek particularism." It is cultural/ethnic particularism, which has no overt religious implication such as divine election or limited redemption. However, the notion that the white stone placed in the inmost sanctuary of Apollo in Delphi is ὁ ὀμφαλός (τῆς γῆς), i.e., the place that Zeus marked as the center of the earth,[10] reveals that ethnic particularism and religious particularism often go hand in hand.

It is not until the Hellenistic period that universalism finds a place in the history of Greek thought. Diogenes Laertius presents the legendary Cynic philosopher Diogenes of Sinope (ca. 404–323 B.C.E.) as the first among Greeks who showed a universalistic perspective. It is said that, when he was asked where he was from, he said, "I am from the universal city."[11] Diogenes is also quoted as having ridiculed such things as good birth (εὐγένεια) and fame (δόξα), which Greeks valued very highly, saying that the only true citizenship should be in the universe.[12] According to Plutarch, Zeno (335–263 B.C.E.), the founder of Stoic philosophy, articulated universalism with the notion of a state (πολιτεία) in which all humankind live as one people with a common law and in a common order.[13] Plutarch further says that it was Alexander the Great (356–323 B.C.E.) who, even before Zeno, actually put the idea of universalism into practice and treated Greeks and foreigners equally, even though his mentor Aristotle had advised him to the contrary.[14] Strabo presents a quotation of the mathematician and geographer Eratosthenes, which says the same thing about Alexander.[15] From these, an image of Alexander the Great emerges as a dreamer of the utopia where all people are united as one race in one culture. One may call it cultural universalism.

This idealized picture of Alexander the Great, which is largely dependent on the statements of Plutarch and Strabo, is perhaps an exaggerated one. However, there is at least some truth in saying that, when Alexander conquered the entire Mediterranean world in the early fourth century B.C.E., he did not try to make it an enlarged version of his Macedonian kingdom. Instead, he wanted to make his entire conquered territory one blended cultural unit, which was conceptualized by such words as ἡ οἰκουμένη (γῆ), meaning "the inhabited land," or ἡ ὁμόνοια, meaning "unity" or "harmony."[16]

It is important to recognize that these new ideas of Stoicism, Cynicism, and the conquest of Alexander were folded together into making the Hellenistic period a new era of universalism, regardless of their relative order of contribution. In this Hellenistic world, the boundaries among nations and ethnic groups tended to blur, and communications and interactions among different cultures became very active and frequent. Because of this international character, the Hellenistic period became the heyday of interactions among religions, and it was in this Hellenistic period that some Mediterranean religions began to engage in missionary ventures. This marks the beginning of universalism in the history of Western religions.

PARTICULARISM AND UNIVERSALISM
IN HEBREW SCRIPTURES

In the history of religions, particularism usually predates universalism, and the religion of Israel was no exception to this. During the periods of the Davidic monarchy and the divided kingdoms, particularism functioned as the organizing principle of theology and political ideology in Israel, as it did in other parts of the world. This does not deny that the seed for universalism was already present in the early sources of the Hebrew Bible.[17] In terms of tradition history, however, the dominant ideology of the religion of preexilic Israel was particularism. There is nothing extraordinary about this, since prior to the Hellenistic period most religions were tribal, nationalistic, and particularistic.

The fundamental logic of Jewish particularism is based on monotheism and election, which were the two major features of Jewish theology. They served as important distinguishing markers of Judaism. Each of the two has its own integrity, but they are also in dialectical relationship with each other. That is, there is only one God, Yahweh, and this Yahweh chose only one people, Israel, and made an exclusive covenant with them. The covenant is that Yahweh alone is the God of Israel, and Israel alone is the chosen people of Yahweh. Thus came the notion that there are two kinds of people in the world: the chosen people of Israel and the Gentiles.[18] This distinction itself, which could be characterized as particularistic, would not necessarily engender exclusivism. However, as a small nation surrounded and frequently threatened by neighboring superpowers, it would not have been easy for Israel to develop a universalistic soteriology, especially when the notion of *shalom* in Israel naturally included deliverance from the predicaments of war with other nations. That is why particularism often resulted in feeding exclusiveness in ancient Israel.

It is not until the period of the Babylonian captivity of the kingdom of Judah that an alternative voice was raised by an anonymous prophet, usually called Deutero-Isaiah, who gave a new interpretation of the traditional notion of election.[19] In his new hermeneutic, the people of Israel were chosen not in order that they alone may be saved but in order that they may become God's instrument through which all the nations can be brought to God.[20] This idea is expressed by the famous metaphor of Israel as a "light to the nations" (Isa. 42:6; 49:6),[21] which became the central symbol of universalism both in later Judaism and Christianity.[22] Deutero-Isaiah thus created an immediate tension with the old paradigm.[23] It marked the beginning of the tension between particularism and universalism in the history of Jewish thought.

The return from Babylon witnessed a resurgence of particularism, which is represented by Ezra and Nehemiah and best exemplified by their divorce decree for those who had married foreign wives (Ezra 9:1–10:44; Neh. 13:23–31). This decree should be seen in the context that it would not have been easy for the leaders of the returned people of Israel to reestablish their religious traditions in the once-destroyed homeland. They would have needed concrete measures to reestablish their national and religious identity. Nevertheless, it was still a drastic measure to dissolve the families of intermarriage and send away the foreign wives and their children (Ezra 10:3, 19, and 44), who, after all, had obediently followed their husbands and fathers to a land completely unknown to them. Only an extreme form of particularism would have been a driving force for such a severe action.

Behind this particularist policy lies a concrete social reality of postexilic Judah in the fifth century B.C.E. Those Palestinian Judahites who had remained and those who repatriated from Babylon would have different political interests. The former would have felt oppressed by the claim to authority of the newcomers from Babylon who represented the Zadokite priestly line.[24] One party would have to prevail over the other in order to achieve sociopolitical stability.[25] As we can see in the Chronicler's history, which is written from the perspective of the repatriates, the newcomers under the leadership of Nehemiah and Ezra, the officials appointed by the Persians, had definite advantage over the Palestinian Judahites. It seems natural that the returning leaders would adopt a particularistic policy as a means to check those who had remained and intermingled with the Samaritan Israelites. If that was the case, the hidden target of the divorce decree could have been those Palestinian Judahites who had married Samaritan women. Thus, particularism as a religious cause reveals a noticeable sociopolitical motivation.

On the other hand, there was also a continuing voice of universalism, as attested by such postexilic books as Ruth and Jonah. The book of Ruth beautifully portrays the life journey of a "foreign" woman, Ruth, who marries an expatriate Israelite, is subsequently widowed, and yet does not leave her mother-in-law but follows her to the land of Israel. The story closes with a happy ending, in which God richly blesses this "foreign" heroine Ruth by having her embraced by another Israelite, Boaz, and thus making her an ancestral matriarch of the royal line of King David (Ruth 4:17). Could this be a parody to the story of the divorce decree of Ezra and Nehemiah? In any case, the book of Ruth clearly advocates universalism in the form of a narrative theology. The book of Jonah is another case of postexilic literature unambiguously advocating universalism. Because of the strong influence of this book on some of the key passages of the New Testament discussed later in this book, it merits an extensive treatment at this point.

JONAH AS A PARADIGMATIC STORY OF UNIVERSALISM

Like any other story, the book of Jonah can be and has been read in many different ways. The issue of whether it is history or fiction is irrelevant here. What is important about this book for us is how the story fits into the larger picture of the tension between universalism and particularism in Judaism. The implied author of the book of Jonah is an adherent of universalism, who chose to advocate it by telling a story in which the main character, Jonah, is a caricature of a Jewish particularist.[26] Using such rhetorical skills as irony, sarcasm, and hyperbole, the narrator of this story subtly reveals the folly of the dogma of particularism.

The story opens with the living voice of God to Jonah, the prophet, telling him to go to Nineveh and cry against it (וּקְרָא עָלֶיהָ), because their wickedness has come up before God (Jonah 1:1–2). Implicit in this command is God's intention for the Ninevehites to listen, repent, and be saved. This would sound completely incomprehensible to certain Jews, like Jonah, who believed that in the exclusive covenant relationship between God and Israel, God is supposed to deal only with Israel. Why should God be concerned about a Gentile nation anyway? Speaking to Gentiles on behalf of God for their deliverance would be against the conventional understanding of the covenant from the perspective of the orthodox particularism. So here is an interesting juxtaposition of an orthodox dogma and the living voice of God. Jonah as a faithful Jewish particularist chooses to adhere to the former. Not having the guts to argue with God, he flees from the presence of God (מִלִּפְנֵי יְהוָה) in order to avoid the theologically incorrect command of God (v. 3). It is telling that Jonah has to go away from the presence of God in order to maintain his orthodox theology.

This opening scene of Jonah implicitly reveals a certain irony: that when a traditional dogma and the living voice of God compete with each other, it is usually the former that wins. In the story of Jonah, God gives the prophet Jonah a commandment that sounds radically new (Jonah 1:2) but Jonah refuses to obey, abiding by the old theology with which he is familiar. So, in a sarcastic portrayal of the tenacity of tradition, God loses and the orthodox theologian wins. In the following scene on the sea, the Gentile sailors are worshipping God, while the disobedient prophet Jonah is thrown into the sea (vv. 14–16),[27] after which peace is restored to the sea. Thus the Gentiles on board are saved while Jonah the Jew is cast out: another instance of a sarcastic twist of the conventional wisdom of Jewish particularism. The following story of a big fish and the song of Jonah in chapter 2 have very little to do with the main theme of the story, and it has been suggested by the majority of scholars that it is a later interpolation.[28]

The rescued prophet Jonah in chapter 3 receives the same command from God again and this time he obeys, although he has not been theologically changed, as the later part of the story shows. It is interesting that there is a statement in verse 3 about the size of Nineveh: "Now Nineveh was an exceedingly large city, a three days' walk across" (מַהֲלַךְ שְׁלֹשֶׁת יָמִים—3:3b). This detail matters only to the degree that, in spite of the large size of the city, Jonah took *only a day's walk* (מַהֲלַךְ יוֹם אֶחָד) to deliver the message (v. 4)! The narrative function of this contrast is to show Jonah's lack of enthusiasm. It is almost as if Jonah proclaimed the message in as meager a voice as possible lest they should listen, repent, and be saved, which echoes with the enigmatic oracle in Isaiah 6:9–10 (cf. Mark 4:11–12).

The story adds still another level of contrast. In spite of Jonah's unenthusiastic delivery of the message, the entire city of Nineveh listens and repents—with the result that all its inhabitants are saved from the impending destruction. The implication is that God's will to save this Gentile city was so great that it led to this kind of miracle. This unconventional act of God infuriates Jonah (Jonah 4:1). So he appeals to God, apparently hoping that God might repent and switch back to the original plan to destroy the city. Having let his wish be known to God, Jonah goes out to the east of the city, sets up a booth, and sits down to see whether God will take his appeal seriously. Obviously Jonah does not think the matter is settled, even after God made the deliberation to save Nineveh. He still wants to see the Gentile city destroyed (v. 5).

God tries to give Jonah a lesson by first providing him with a bush that gives him shade and then taking it away. In another fit of anger Jonah again protests to God (4:8). Then, like a patient teacher God asks Jonah:

> You are concerned about the bush, for which you did not labor and which you did not grow; it came into being in a night and perished in a night. And should I not be concerned about Nineveh, that great city, in which there are more than a hundred and twenty thousand persons who do not know their right hand from their left, and also many animals? (Jonah 4:10–11)

The narrative ends with this rhetorical question of God. Has God succeeded in persuading Jonah? Has Jonah learned a lesson from God? The text is silent about that, but most probably the implication of the silence of the narrative is that Jonah has still not been persuaded. By ending the story this way, the author of the book of Jonah seems to be alluding to the position of the adamant particularists of that time, who would not listen to God's new voice because it did not conform to conventional theology. In that sense, Jonah is a caricature of those conventionalists. The ending of this story may reflect the harsh reality that it is very difficult to convert theologically convinced particularists into universalists.

It is not easy to locate the provenance and the date of the book of Jonah. Judging from the implicit critique of the author against the particularistic understanding of the divine grace, however, one could put it either contemporaneous with the final redactor of the Chronicles or shortly afterwards. This suggests that, just as Nehemiah and Ezra advocated an exclusivist and particularist ethos in trying to reconstruct the Jewish nation/religion with the temple as its center and the Torah as its constitution, there were wisdom teachers whose horizon was more international and universalistic. The prophetic universalism of Jonah, reflecting the influence of Deutero-Isaiah, would squarely fit the latter category.[29]

CONTINUED TENSION IN POST-BIBLICAL JUDAISM

With such books as Ezra, Nehemiah, Jonah, and Ruth, we observe the unresolved tension between particularism and universalism in Jewish society around the last period accounted for by the canonical Hebrew Scripture.[30] From there one could naturally assume that the tension continued further into the intertestamental period, which is indeed the case. That is, there existed in Second Temple Judaism a spectrum of opinions concerning the issue of the salvation of the Gentiles, and literature can be cited both for particularism and for universalism.[31] For example, *Jubilees,* which is generally dated in the middle of the second century B.C.E., testifies to an extreme form of particularism. According to this document, anyone who was not circumcised on the eighth day belongs outside the covenant and therefore among the children of destruction.

> And anyone who is born whose own flesh is not circumcised on the eighth day is not from the sons of the covenant which the Lord made for Abraham since (he is) from the children of destruction. And there is therefore no sign upon him so that he might belong to the Lord because (he is destined) to be destroyed and annihilated from the earth and to be uprooted from the earth because he has broken the covenant of the Lord our God. (*Jub.* 15:26–27)[32]

This makes Gentile conversion virtually impossible, because one ought to have been circumcised on the eighth day from birth.[33] More importantly, this text presupposes a sharp dichotomy between the sons of the covenant and the children of destruction. It also says there will be sons of Israel who will not observe the ordinance of circumcision and they will be destroyed just like the uncircumcised Gentiles (*Jub.* 15:33–34). This is a highly sectarian mentality that categorically declares there is no salvation without circumcision.[34]

In contrast, Pseudo-Phocylides, usually dated in the first century B.C.E. to the first century C.E., represents a markedly universalistic tendency. The book opens with what seems to be a truncated version of the Decalogue (3–8), and conspicuously missing from here are the first four commandments of the Decalogue, which are the most particularly Jewish in nature. Then the main body of admonitions emphasizes such universal virtues as justice (9–21), mercy (22–41), honesty (48–50), self-control (57–58), and moderation (59–69). The book ends with a summary statement that says, "Purifications are for the purity of the soul, not of the body" (228). So the whole notion of the ritual purity of Israel and the separation of Israel from the Gentile nations plays virtually no role in this document. The Jewish *Sibylline Oracles*, roughly contemporary with Pseudo-Phocylides, also specifies moral injunction for all humanity, through which Gentiles could become righteous.[35]

The parallel existence of particularism and universalism still continues down to rabbinic literature, which was actually written from the third to sixth century C.E. but which may contain traditions going back to as early as the first century B.C.E. Among the possibly early traditions, the best-known example of the tension of the two different theologies is the debate between the two competing rabbinic schools in Jerusalem: Beth Shammai (בת שמי) and Beth Hillel (בת הלל). Both Shammai and Hillel are teachers of the Torah in Jerusalem in the first century B.C.E. and possibly in the first decade of the first century C.E. In the rabbinic traditions, the former appears to represent conservative particularism and the latter more progressive and open-minded universalism. A well-known anecdote in the Babylonian Talmud exemplifies the difference between the two with regard to their basic attitudes toward Gentiles:

> It happened that a certain heathen came before Shammai and said to him, "Make me a proselyte, on condition that you teach me the whole Torah while I stand on one foot." Thereupon he repulsed him with the builder's cubit which was in his hand. When he went before Hillel, he said to him, "What is hateful to you, do not to your neighbour (דעלך סני לחברך לא תעביד): That is the whole Torah, while the rest is the commentary thereof; go and learn it."[36]

There are many other similar stories in the same tractate, which clearly show two different theological tendencies concerning the relation between Jews and Gentiles—tendencies that continued to exist during and after New Testament times. While it is possible that such a debate was retrospectively put into the mouths of the earlier teachers of the Law by the Amoraic editors, the tension between particularism and universalism is attested for much earlier periods in other literature including biblical writings. Therefore I think it is highly probable that such a tension also existed during the time of Hillel and Shammai.

The two different attitudes toward Gentiles in Jewish society had a significant implication for the question of the status of Gentiles with regard to salvation. On the one hand, there was the idea that in the days of Yahweh's salvation "the uncircumcised and the unclean" (עָרֵל וְטָמֵא) will be forbidden to enter the holy city, Jerusalem (Isa. 52:1). The rationale behind this categorical statement is the premise that what is impure is detestable (שֶׁקֶץ) to Yahweh (Lev. 11:43–47) and therefore should be shunned from the presence of Yahweh. While Hebrew Scripture does not contain a specific statement that Gentiles, as such, are impure, the prohibition of Gentiles from entering the temple of Jerusalem may potentially imply that they were regarded as impure. It is in that vein that the Tractate *Makkot* of the Babylonian Talmud categorically calls Gentiles impure persons,[37] and that *Jubilees* gives a clear injunction not to associate or eat with Gentiles because of their uncleanness.[38] Another example can be cited from *Mekilta Mishpatim* 10, in which R. Ishmael says, "So also in the future world there will be some for whom there will be redemption and there will be some for whom there will be no redemption. For the heathen nations there will be no redemption."[39] This passage further entertains the idea that the Israelites are blessed because Yahweh has given the heathen nations of the world as ransom for their souls!

A further development of this idea is the negative soteriological implication of being *uncircumcised*. That is, at one extreme of the spectrum, there are some passages in rabbinic literature that postulate uncircumcised Gentiles will not be saved. For example, there is a story in midrash about a "God-fearing" Roman senator who, at the advice of his "righteous" wife, gave his life to protect the Jews against a decree of expulsion. Here is an excerpt of the passage in which the rabbis speak with the bereaved wife of the Roman senator:

> When the Rabbis heard of it they came to his wife to express their sympathy. The Rabbis said to her, "Alas for the ship that has sailed without paying her dues" (meaning thereby, that this righteous man [her husband] had not been circumcised). Said his wife to them, "I fully understand the meaning of what you say; by your life, before the ship sailed, she did pay her dues." Immediately she entered the chamber and brought out thence unto them a box wherein was the foreskin with rags full of blood upon it. The Rabbis thereupon applied to him [her husband] the following Scriptural verse, The princes of the peoples are gathered together, the people of the God of Abraham; for unto God belong the shields of the earth. He is greatly exalted (Ps. XLVII, 10).[40]

Thus, it was only after they saw the evidence for the deceased Roman senator to have been circumcised that they assured the wife that he had been saved. This story reveals an unmistakably particularistic soteriology, in which salvation is only for the covenant people, for whom circumcision is the critical marker. In such a particularistic soteriology, circumcision matters not as a ritual per se but as a marker of the covenant people, for whom alone salvation is reserved.

On the other hand, there were other rabbis who had a completely different understanding of the soteriological status of some, if not all, Gentiles who had not been proselytized into accepting Judaism through circumcision. They believed that some uncircumcised Gentiles would be regarded as righteous and saved. It is interesting to find in one and the same passage in Tosefta a close juxtaposition of two different opinions concerning the status of Gentiles in the world to come:

> R. Eliezer says, "None of the gentiles has a portion in the world to come, as it is said, *The wicked shall return to Sheol, all the gentiles who forget God* (Ps. 9:17)." . . . Said to him R. Joshua, "If it had been written, '*The wicked shall return to Sheol—all the gentiles*' and then said nothing further, I should have maintained as you do. Now that it is in fact written, *All the gentiles who forget God*, it indicates that there also are righteous people among the nations of the world, who do have a portion in the world to come."[41] (italics added)

Thus, in this passage R. Joshua presents his universalistic soteriology in no ambiguous terms, which is the main point of the cited Tosefta text.

There is another passage from the Babylonian Talmud that has a similar juxtaposition. R. Eliezer is also quoted in *Baba Bathra* as saying, "All the charity and kindness done by the heathen is counted to them as sin, because they only do it to magnify themselves." In contrast, at the conclusion of the same Talmudic passage, R. Johanan b. Zakkai says, "Just as the sin-offering makes atonement for Israel, so charity makes atonement for the heathen."[42] Here again Johanan b. Zakkai's universalistic soteriology is the main point that the Talmudic text drives.

A still different tractate of the Babylonian Talmud contains another case of contrast concerning the attitude toward Gentiles. R. Johanan said, "A heathen (נכרי lit. foreigner) who studies the Torah deserves death, for it is written, 'Moses commanded us a law for an inheritance.' It is our inheritance, not theirs."[43] In still another tractate of the Babylonian Talmud, however, R. Meir said, "Whence can we learn that even where a gentile (נכרי) occupies himself with the study of the Torah he equals the High Priest?"[44] Thus, in those cited passages, Rabbis Eliezer and Johanan epitomize particularistic soteriology, whereas Rabbis Joshua, Johanan b. Zakkai, and Meir represent universalistic soteriology.

Another important rabbinic tradition concerning the status of Gentiles is the Noachian Commandments, which are listed in a number of rabbinic writings (e.g., T. *Abodah Zarah* 8.4, B. *Sanhedrin* 56ab, *Genesis Rabbah* 16.6, *Song of Songs Rabbah* 1.2). They are universal ethical commandments for the Gentiles who are not converted to Judaism.[45] There were debates among rabbis on how many and what kinds of commandments there were in the Noachian Law[46] and what the exact implications of them were.[47] We also do not know how widely the notion of the Noachian Law was accepted in Judaism. However, the multiple attestations of it in various types of rabbinic literature testify to a fairly strong universalistic tradition in Judaism—at least, in the Tannaitic and Amoraic periods—which acknowledged the possibility for uncircumcised Gentiles to become righteous and thus to be saved by observing the universal commandments.

In conclusion, these diverse examples from rabbinic literature, even though their dating is extremely difficult, give evidence of the existence of different and often conflicting views concerning the salvation of the uncircumcised Gentiles among Jewish thinkers throughout the rabbinic periods. Thus, it is important to recognize that there is no justification for any sweeping generalization about the Jewish attitude toward Gentiles, because there would have been competing opinions among the Jews at any given moment of their history concerning the salvation of the Gentiles. The traditional Christian stereotype of "particularistic Judaism and universalistic Christianity" is a gross misrepresentation of both. Earliest Christianity, which was a Jewish sect, reflected a tension between particularism and universalism that already existed in the larger part of Judaism. It is against this backdrop that early Christian debates concerning Gentile mission arose and developed.

Chapter 2

The Beginning
of Early Christianity

TWO DIFFERENT ACCOUNTS OF THE BEGINNING

Contrary to what is generally assumed, it is extremely difficult to know how early Christianity started after Jesus and whether or not it had direct historical/theological connection with the historical Jesus.[1] First of all, there are different accounts in the New Testament about what exactly happened to Jesus after the resurrection. According to Acts, Jesus stayed in and around Jerusalem for forty days after his resurrection and then he ascended into heaven. This straightforward account of the actions of the resurrected Jesus, however, raises a number of questions.

Here one should note that Acts 1:9–11 is the only place in the New Testament where the ascension of Jesus is narrated as a separate event from his resurrection.[2] Paul never mentions the ascension of Jesus, and the tradition he cites in 1 Corinthians 15:1–3 lists the death, burial, and resurrection of Christ but not his ascension. Mark ends his story of Jesus with the empty tomb narrative (Mark 16:1–8). Matthew has a post-Easter christophany narrative (Matt. 28:16–20), but the text does not say he "ascended" into heaven. Unlike Acts 1:9–11, Matthew 28:16–20 does not describe how Jesus departed but, paradoxically, how he in fact did *not* depart. That is, the Matthean Jesus says to his disciples that he will always be with them until the end of ages (Matt. 28:20). Hence there is no room or need for the ascension of Jesus in the Gospel of Matthew.[3]

Perhaps the common assumption behind all these canonical accounts about what happened to the resurrected Jesus, except in Luke–Acts, was that the resurrection of Jesus and his exaltation to the right hand of God happened simultaneously. The pericope of the resurrection of Jesus in the *Gospel of Peter* is more explicit about this idea:

> While they were telling what they had seen, they again saw three men coming out of the tomb, the two (of them) supporting the other and a cross following them. (They saw) the heads of the two extending to heaven and that of the one who was being led by them overpassing the heavens. And they heard a voice from heaven, saying, "Did you preach to those who were sleeping?" And a response was heard from the cross, "Yes."[4]

So the chronological sequence of the resurrection, the ascension, Pentecost, and the foundation of the Christian church in Jerusalem may not reflect a common understanding among early Christians regarding historical reality, but rather Luke's historicizing tendency.[5]

Second, the canonical Gospels attest to two conflicting traditions concerning the whereabouts of the disciples of Jesus after the resurrection. First, Mark 16:7 presents an announcement to the disciples that Jesus is going ahead of them to Galilee, as he previously told them. Thus, Galilee is the designated place for the reunion between the resurrected Jesus and his disciples in Mark. Even though the actual story line of Mark stops short there, the authorial intention would be that the reader assumes the prophecy in Mark 16:7, like all others in the Gospel, was indeed fulfilled in the untold part of the story. This would mean that the disciples went back to Galilee, where they indeed encountered Jesus as risen, and that they started witnessing to their faith in the resurrected Jesus there in Galilee. In other words, early Christianity began *in Galilee*. This scenario would fit well with the natural expectation that those Jews who came to Jerusalem to observe one of the pilgrim festivals, such as the Passover, would naturally go back to their hometowns when the festival was over. The disciples were Galileans, and so they went back to Galilee.[6]

Matthew follows this tradition of Mark, keeping Galilee as the place of the reunion between Jesus and his disciples. Matthew 28:7, for example, preserves Mark 16:7 almost verbatim. Then Matthew adds another pericope, in which the risen Jesus appears to the women on their way to the disciples (Matt. 28:8–10). There Matthew inserts a saying of Jesus in the form of an explicit command to the disciples to go back to Galilee (v. 10). Matthew 28:16–20 then indicates the disciples indeed followed the command of Jesus and the prophecy was fulfilled. That is, the disciples went back to Galilee, and it is on a mountain *in Galilee* (v. 16) that they encountered the resurrected Jesus. Thus in the Gospel of Matthew, Galilee remains as the place of origin of early Christianity.

It is very interesting to compare Luke's redaction on the same Markan passage with that of Matthew. First of all, Luke completely deletes Mark 16:7, which is the prophecy of the reunion between Jesus and his disciples in Galilee. In Luke, Jesus does not appear to the women who went to the tomb at the dawn of Easter, as he does in Matthew. Instead, he appears to two anonymous disciples on the way to Emmaus, which is in the vicinity of *Jerusalem* (Luke 24:13–32). Then Jesus also appears to the eleven disciples in *Jerusalem* (v. 33). There he specifically commands his disciples to remain in *Jerusalem* (v. 49). Later, in Acts 1:4, this command of Jesus to his disciples not to leave Jerusalem is repeated. The ascension of Jesus itself takes place on Mount Olivet, which Luke says is "near Jerusalem" (Acts 1:12), and after the ascension the disciples return to Jerusalem. There, pursuant to the command of Jesus (Luke 24:49), they remain in Jerusalem (Acts 1:13). It is *in Jerusalem* that they receive the Holy Spirit on the day of Pentecost and begin witnessing to their faith. In other words, in the narrative world of Luke–Acts, early Christianity began in *Jerusalem*, not in Galilee.[7]

Considering the late date of Luke and his tendency to highlight the special meaning of Jerusalem throughout his Gospel and Acts, one wonders whether this tradition of Jerusalem as the exclusive place of the post-Easter encounter of Jesus and his disciples (and as the birthplace of the "post-Jesus" Jesus movement) was created by the redactional hand of Luke. Of course, it is possible that Luke did not invent this tradition but drew on an earlier source that already had Jerusalem as the place of origin of early Christianity. If that is the case, the putative earlier source was permanently lost. Also, even if there was an earlier source behind the Lukan version of the beginning of early Christianity in Jerusalem, the early date of the pre-Lukan source alone does not necessarily establish the historicity of the tradition it represents.

This conflict of information in the gospel corpus about where early Christianity began cannot easily be resolved. It cautions us that what happened in the very first chapter of early Christian history may not be known with any degree of certainty.[8] However, that should not lead us to excessive skepticism regarding what Acts has to say about the early leaders of the Jerusalem church. After all, in Galatians 1:18 Paul independently attests to the fact that Peter was indeed *in Jerusalem* when he visited there for the first time after his conversion. The following two verses (Gal. 1:19–20) imply that Paul expected Peter and the other apostles to be in Jerusalem when he visited there, and that it was a common assumption that the apostles were all in Jerusalem at that time. To his surprise, however, Paul did not find any other apostle than Peter when he arrived at the Jerusalem church. Does this mean that the other apostles had been there previously but had already left? Or does it mean that they had never even been there? We are as puzzled about that as Paul implies he was.

In any case, Pauline chronology, as it is calculated backward from the Gallio inscription, which is supposed to overlap with Paul's Corinthian ministry, tells us that Paul's visit to Jerusalem mentioned in Galatians 1:18 was around 35 C.E., which must have been only a few years after the crucifixion of Jesus. That means, regardless of whether the disciples of Jesus went back to Galilee or remained in Jerusalem immediately after the crucifixion of Jesus, at least one of them—Peter—was found to be present in Jerusalem as early as the mid-30s C.E.

According to what Paul says in Galatians 2:1–10, when he went up to Jerusalem again "fourteen years later," which would have been around 49 C.E., Peter and John, together with James the Lord's brother, were found to be present in Jerusalem as the "pillars" of the Jewish Christian community (Gal. 2:9). If it is true that the visit of Paul to Jerusalem mentioned in Galatians 2:1 was in connection with the Apostolic Council in Jerusalem, as I believe it was, then the text's counterpart in Acts 15 verifies what Paul says in Galatians 2:9 about the presence of Peter and James the Lord's brother at the Jerusalem church. In this case, it is not clear whether Peter was there as a resident member/leader of the Jerusalem church or whether he was invited back to Jerusalem to attend the special meeting. I will come back to this point later.

For now, it is important to note that the presence of at least two important disciples of Jesus, Peter and John, in Jerusalem in the mid-30s to late 40s C.E. is established by a primary source (Galatians) and its partial coherence with a secondary one (Acts). From here, in the absence of evidence contrary to what Acts says, we may further entertain the possibility that all or some of the other members of the Twelve might also have been there in the Jerusalem church at or before the Apostolic Council in Jerusalem.[9] If that is the case, it is not unreasonable to assume that the disciples of Jesus played a significant leadership role in the Jerusalem church from the beginning, even though we do not know exactly when or how the church started.[10] In that sense, one could say that the Jerusalem church as the apostolic church had at least some historical, if not theological, continuity with the historical Jesus.

THE JERUSALEM CHURCH

It has been pointed out that as early as the mid-30s C.E. Peter and some other apostles were active leaders of the Jerusalem church. What is not clear is their theological outlook, especially concerning the scope of their mission. Early chapters of Acts present Peter and John as witnessing to their faith in Jesus as the Messiah. Their intended audience was Jews, as clearly indicated by the address "You Israelites" in Peter's sermon in Acts 3:12. According to Acts 11:19, those who were scattered from Jerusalem preached *only to the Jews*, from which we can infer that the apostles who remained in Jerusalem had also preached only to the Jews. Was limiting the targeted audience to Jews only a temporary measure based upon the multi-staged universal mission plan in Acts 1:8? Even though that is what the author of Acts seems to imply, it is not to be taken for granted in terms of historicity. By the same token, even though the Lukan Peter says, "[Jesus] must remain in heaven until the time for the restoration of *all people*" (ἄχρι χρόνων ἀποκαταστάσεως πάντων, Acts 3:21, my translation), it is highly questionable that the historical Peter had such a universalistic soteriological vision in the earlier period of his apostleship.

What is more probable is that Peter and the other apostles understood Jesus as the Messiah for the Jews, so they proclaimed their kerygma to their fellow Jews only. That is perfectly understandable because it was only natural for Jews to understand the meaning of the word *Messiah* in terms of the restoration of the Davidic kingdom. If the Caesarea Philippi pericope in Mark 8:27–38 has any historical nucleus, it would be the disciples' (mis)understanding of Jesus as the

Messiah who would restore the Davidic kingdom to Israel—an idea clearly articulated in this pericope by Peter as the disciples' spokesperson. According to Mark, even after Jesus' repeated attempts at correcting it (Mark 8:31; 9:31; 10:33), this kind of messianic expectation continued to dominate the disciples' minds, as the request of the sons of Zebedee for Jesus to reserve seats of honor and power for them in the restored kingdom (Mark 10:35–45) tellingly testifies.

Acts 1:6 also supports the idea that the disciples understood Jesus as one who would restore the Davidic kingdom to Israel. Probably their expectation would have reached the highest point when they believed that by raising Jesus from the dead God had just proved that Jesus was the Messiah. So, could there be a better time than now for Jesus the Messiah to accomplish what he was supposed to accomplish (Acts 1:6)? In the story line of Acts, this particularist Christology/soteriology represents the original understanding of the disciples, which is to be corrected later in the story.[11]

Whatever its beginning was like, the Jerusalem church did not turn out to be a homogeneous group. Acts 6:1–7 talks about two parties in the church, the Hebrews (οἱ Ἑβραῖοι) and the Hellenists (οἱ Ἑλληνισταί), who did not get along. The text says that there was a grievance from the widows of the Hellenists against the Hebrews concerning the daily distribution of food, but the matter seems to be more serious than that. In his pivotal work on Paul,[12] F. C. Baur correctly argues that there was a long-standing theological dissension between the Hebrews and the Hellenists within the Jerusalem church, which eventually led to the institution of the new office of the seven leaders from the Hellenists.[13] Baur further points out that the persecution against the Jerusalem church was chiefly against the Hellenists, who, as Stephen's speech indicates, were critical about the Jerusalem temple cult, while the Hebrews adhered to it.[14] Baur believes that this persecution widened the gap between the two factions in the Jerusalem church and that eventually the Hellenists left Jerusalem and the Hebrews remained. This is when the Jerusalem church became more adamant about observing the temple cult and about subscribing to the theology that supported it. The result is that the Jerusalem church became even more particularistic in their scope of mission. In contrast, those Hellenistic Jewish Christians who left the Jerusalem church because of the persecution spread more broadly and expanded their mission scope.[15]

Martin Hengel says it is remarkable that only shortly after the resurrection the proclamation of the crucified and resurrected Jesus attracted the Greek-speaking Jews, who came from diverse cultural backgrounds of the Diaspora and settled in Jerusalem. For him, this aspect of the Christian message that transcended the boundaries of language and culture is what distinguished early Christianity from the other Palestinian Jewish movements.[16] Soon after leaving Jerusalem, these Greek-speaking Jewish Christians began their missionary preaching with a more universalistic outlook. Fertile soil for universal mission was being prepared.

THE "CONVERSION" OF PAUL

Reconstructing the life of Paul is almost as difficult as the quest for the historical Jesus.[17] The fact that we have Paul's own writings certainly puts the venture of writing a biography of Paul in a different category than that of Jesus or Socrates, who left no writings of their own. However, none of Paul's writings are primarily autobiographical, and even those sections of the Epistles that can be regarded as "autobiographical" usually have different rhetorical functions than to be informative. The question of the reliability of Acts as a historical document has long been discussed in New Testament scholarship, and scholarly opinion varies along a full spectrum ranging from cautious but favorable assessment to radical skepticism.[18]

Writing a biography of Paul is not the purpose of this book, let alone establishing an exact chronology of his life. However, in order to put him in the larger picture of early Christian mission, we need at least a working hypothesis for the course of Paul's life, especially as it relates to the conflicts between universalism and particularism in early Christianity. In this tentative reconstruction, the sequence of events, not their exact dates, is important for the main argument of this book.

30 C.E.	The crucifixion of Jesus
32 C.E.	The conversion of Paul
35 C.E.	Paul's first visit to Jerusalem
49 C.E.	The Apostolic Council at Jerusalem
50 C.E.	The Antioch Incident
51–53 C.E.	Paul's stay in Corinth (1 Thessalonians and Galatians)
53–56 C.E.	Paul's stay in Ephesus (1–2 Corinthians)
57 C.E.	Paul's stay in Macedonia and Corinth (Romans)
58 C.E.	Paul's collection visit to Jerusalem
58–60 C.E.	Imprisonment in Caesarea
60 C.E.	Paul's journey to Rome
60–62 C.E.	Imprisonment in Rome (Philemon and Philippians)
62 C.E.	Martyrdom of Paul

All figures are approximate years.

About his life before the conversion,[19] Paul has the following to say:

> If anyone else has reason to be confident in the flesh, I have more: circumcised on the eighth day, a member of the people of Israel, of the tribe of Benjamin, a Hebrew born of Hebrews; as to the law, a Pharisee; as to zeal, a persecutor of the church; as to righteousness under the law, blameless. (Phil. 3:4b–6)

and

> You have heard, no doubt, of my earlier life in Judaism. I was violently per-
> secuting the church of God and was trying to destroy it. I advanced in
> Judaism beyond many among my people of the same age, for I was far more
> zealous for the traditions of my ancestors. (Gal. 1:13–14)

Also, the Lukan Paul says,

> I am a Jew, born in Tarsus in Cilicia, but brought up in this city at the feet
> of Gamaliel, educated strictly according to our ancestral law, being zealous
> for God, just as all of you are today. I persecuted this Way up to the point
> of death by binding both men and women and putting them in prison, as
> the high priest and the whole council of elders can testify about me. (Acts
> 22:3–5a)

The first two Pauline passages cited above come from highly polemical contexts
and therefore one needs to be cautious about taking them at face value. Also, the
speech of Paul in Acts 22:3–21 is a Lukan composition, and therefore the veracity of its content can not simply be assumed.[20]

However, a few basic facts can be deduced from these passages. First of all, Paul
was born a Jew of the tribe of Benjamin. The information that Paul was born in
Tarsus comes only from Acts. However, we may safely assume that it is correct,
because Luke would have no particular reason to fabricate this information.[21]
Paul's earlier contemporary Strabo, probably with some exaggeration, says, "The
people at Tarsus have devoted themselves so eagerly, not only to philosophy, but
also to the whole round of education in general, that they have surpassed Athens,
Alexandria, or any other place that can be named where there have been schools
and lectures of philosophers" (14.5.13).[22] Indeed in the first century B.C.E. Tarsus
was a "university town," i.e., one of the centers of philosophical as well as rhetorical schools[23] that attracted students from all over the Mediterranean region and
that would have promoted cosmopolitanism based on the Hellenistic idea of universalism. What bearing does this fact have on our understanding of Paul? Even if
it is true that Paul was born in Tarsus, we do not even know how long he lived
there. We can only say that if he received his primary and secondary education in
Tarsus, which is not unlikely, he may very well have been richly nurtured for the
Hellenistic idea of the universality of humankind in his youth.

The question of whether Paul studied under Gamaliel is very difficult to set-
tle. Again, it is only in Acts that this connection between Paul and Gamaliel is
made. Knox disputes this Lukan tradition for two reasons. First, Paul never mentions Gamaliel, even when he would have benefited from claiming his connection to him as his former mentor. Second, this connection does serve Luke's
redactional concern to make Christianity a legitimate heir to Judaism.[24] Both reasons suggested by Knox have some truth, but neither should be taken as a decisive argument against the historical veracity of the Lukan account. After all,
Knox's first reason is an argument from silence and his second does not prove that
Luke made up the story. On the other hand, Riesner recently pointed out that
Paul's exegesis of the Old Testament passages reveals a high degree of scholarly

training and therefore indirectly supports the Lukan claim that he was a disciple of Gamaliel.[25] Here also, even though Paul's exegesis may indirectly support the idea that he had some training in Jewish scriptural interpretation, it certainly does not prove Paul's direct connection with Gamaliel.

According to the Babylonian Talmud (*Shabbath* 15a), the four great successive teachers—Hillel, Simeon, Gamaliel, and another Simeon—wielded their patriarchy as Nasi.[26] If this tradition is historically correct, Gamaliel stands in the great tradition of the universalism of Hillel vis-à-vis the particularistic tradition of Shammai.[27] This means that if Acts 22:3 is historical, Paul was trained in the rabbinic tradition that was universalistic with regard to the question of the Gentiles. Taking due caution about the reliability of these traditions, we may not be able to claim too high a degree of historicity for this chain of connection from Hillel to Gamaliel, and from Gamaliel to Paul. The most we can say about it is that the connection makes sense, especially because both Hillel and Paul represent universalism in their respective traditions.

Paul says he was a persecutor of the church (Gal. 1:14; 1 Cor. 15:9; Phil. 3:6). As a Pharisee who was "blameless" (ἄμεμπτος) with regard to the law, Paul might well have had a problem with the Hellenists in the Jerusalem church, who were highly critical of the current religious leadership's understanding of the law and the temple cult.[28] Put in this context, the account in Acts 7:58, in which Saul appears as one among the supporting witnesses of the execution of Stephen, is not entirely incoherent with Paul's own statement of his past persecution of the church in Philippians 3:6, even though it does not mean the account is historical.

There is still another statement of Paul that could be regarded as a piece of biographical information: "But my friends, why am I still being persecuted if I am still preaching circumcision?" (Gal. 5:11a). This is a very difficult passage to interpret. The Greek sentence with the adverb ἔτι ("still") in front of the verb "preach" (εἰ περιτομὴν ἔτι κηρύσσω, τί ἔτι διώκομαι) may imply that he once preached circumcision.[29] Does that mean he was a Jewish missionary to the Gentiles prior to his becoming a believer in Jesus? Some scholars suppose so.[30] If this is the case, we have an important piece of information concerning Paul's pre-Christian theological outlook. Since "preaching circumcision" to Jews would make no sense, the intended audience of Paul's supposed missionary preaching would have been Gentiles.[31] The sheer fact that Paul was interested in preaching to Gentiles would reflect his universalistic tendency, which is well represented by the Hillelian tradition to which he may have belonged, if his Gamaliel connection is historical. In that case, Paul had already been a universalist in the Jewish sense of the word, even before he embraced the gospel of Jesus.

In contrast to the graphic descriptions in Acts (9:1–29; 22:3–21; 26:9–20), Paul himself provides no narrative account of his conversion.[32] What comes closest is the following passage:

> But when God, who had set me apart before I was born and called me through his grace, was pleased to reveal his Son to me, so that I might proclaim him among the Gentiles . . . (Gal. 1:15–16)

Paul here uses the language of prophetic call (καλέσας) and revelation (ἀποκαλύψαι) to describe the change that happened to him. The content of this "revelation" was the vision of Jesus as God's son, and the call was for Gentile mission. It is probably this vision that Paul keeps referring to whenever he says he has seen the Lord (1 Cor. 9:1; 15:8). In other words, Paul understood his encounter with Jesus as a post-Easter christophany.[33] For him this vision of the resurrected Jesus served as evidence that, having been raised from the dead, Jesus had been authenticated as the Son of God (Rom. 1:4). More importantly, for Paul, it legitimized his claim to apostleship, even though other people, especially his opponents, would not acknowledge it.

It is very important to recognize that Paul understood the call to be for a specific mission, i.e., to proclaim the gospel of Jesus *among the Gentiles* (ἵνα εὐαγγελίζωμαι αὐτὸν ἐν τοῖς ἔθνεσιν). So, instead of going to the Jews first and moving to the Gentiles only when the Jews rejected him, which is the picture we get from Acts, Paul himself says he went directly to the Gentiles immediately after his conversion. This would have been natural for him, because he was already standing in the universalistic tradition of Deutero-Isaiah, the Book of Jonah, Hillel, and Gamaliel—and therefore, even before his conversion, he had no doubt that Gentiles were within the purview of God's salvation. Having seen the vision of the resurrected Jesus and having been called to preach him among the Gentiles, Paul now saw the universal soteriological horizon in Jesus, who he previously thought was a lawbreaker. His previous universalism found new terms of articulation in the personally encountered messianic figure of Jesus, the crucified and risen Christ. The seeds for serious conflict with the particularist Jewish Christians in Jerusalem were already there in Paul's own interpretation of his vision.[34]

THE "CONVERSION" OF PETER

If we use the term "conversion" in the sense of critical change of mind (μετάνοια < μετά + νοῦς), there are two paradigmatic conversion stories in Acts: the conversion of Paul in chapter 9[35] and the conversion of Peter in chapter 10.[36] It does not seem to be a coincidence that the two stories are placed side by side in Acts. In terms of the theme, both conversions are closely related to the motif of universalism. The former is a conversion of a non-Christian Jewish universalist into a Christian Jewish universalist; the latter is a conversion of a Christian Jewish particularist into a Christian Jewish universalist.[37] The result is that, at least in the narrative world of Acts, the two paradigmatic leaders of early Christianity end up having the same theological outlook (i.e., Christian Jewish universalism). Even though we see a clear redactional/theological tendency of Luke in operation here, there is no compelling reason to doubt that Peter and Paul eventually came to take the same theological stance with regard to the nature and scope of Christian mission.[38]

There is a striking similarity between the opening of the story of Jonah in the Old Testament and that of Peter in Acts 10. Both Jonah and Peter hear a command from God,[39] which has something to do with the relation of Jews and Gentiles. This connection to the question of Gentiles is stated overtly in Jonah 1:1 and covertly (but unmistakably implied) in Acts 10:11–13. In both cases the command of God runs counter to the traditional understanding of the place of Gentiles in God's dealings with humans, and for that very reason neither Jonah nor Peter obeys it.

The heavenly voice in the story of Peter accompanies a vision (ὅραμα, Acts 10:17), in which a large sheet is let down containing all kinds of unclean animals. The voice then commands Peter to kill and eat the animals, which is obviously against the purity law. So Peter categorically refuses (Μηδαμῶς, κύριε, Acts 10:14) saying that he has never eaten anything profane or unclean (πᾶν κοινὸν καὶ ἀκάθαρτον, v. 14).[40] It goes without saying that the unclean animals in this vision symbolize the Gentiles, as the literary context (vv. 1–8) clearly indicates. Then the voice says, "What God has made clean, you must not call profane" (v. 15).

Considering the significance of the purity law in Judaism at that time, this statement of the heavenly voice is a remarkable one.[41] The point here is that God has launched a new era of salvation, in which there is no longer a soteriologically meaningful distinction between Jews and Gentiles. That is beyond the grasp of the version of traditional Jewish theology that Peter understood. The voice is an invitation for Peter to recognize this dimension of God's freedom to do new things. Peter, however, being too sure about his theological position, is not persuaded. So, the sheet is drawn up with God's command unfulfilled. The adamant theologian wins and God loses. This happens three times, showing the tenacity of old tradition. At least in this section of the story, Peter is a caricature of an adamant traditionalist, just like Jonah. Both in the story of Jonah and that of Peter, when a dogmatic position—especially one believed to be based on the Torah— is at odds with the living voice of God, the former prevails. It is a poignant irony that is unmistakably recognizable in the eyes of a perceptive reader of the stories of Jonah and Peter. This irony is the very essence of the intertexuality between the two stories.

The motif of the tension between written codes and spoken revelation is not without parallel in rabbinic writings. There is an interesting anecdote in the Babylonian Talmud, in which the written Torah is given more weight than a heavenly voice. The context of the anecdote is a theological debate between R. Eliezer and other sages (חכמים) concerning cleanness. When other sages do not accept Eliezer's opinion, he appeals to various miracles as a sign of proof of his argument. When the sages refuse to approve the miracles as acceptable, he finally appeals to a heavenly voice (בת קול, lit. "daughter of the voice"), which responds, saying, "Why do ye dispute with R. Eliezer, seeing that in all matters the halachah agrees with him!" But the adamant R. Joshua still rejects it. R. Jeremiah interprets R. Joshua's rejection as meaning: "The Torah had already been given at Mount Sinai; we pay no attention to a Heavenly Voice (בת קול), because Thou hast long since written in the Torah at Mount Sinai." The other rabbis end up excommunicating R. Eliezer.[42] The same principle is operative in the initial reactions of Jonah and of Peter, although in these cases it is presented sarcastically by the authors, for whom the living voice of God is indeed the channel through which God's new way of salvation is revealed.

Unlike Jonah, Peter in Acts later lets himself be puzzled about the vision he just saw, and he subsequently understands the point of the heavenly voice through the aid of the Spirit (Acts 10:17–20). In the immediately following episode, Peter is invited by a God-fearing Gentile (φοβούμενος τὸν θεόν, v. 22), Cornelius, and accepts the invitation without scruple, because he now begins to see God's new way of salvation. As he enters Cornelius's house, Peter says, "You yourselves know that it is unlawful for a Jew to associate with or to visit a Gentile; but God has shown me that I should not call anyone profane or unclean" (v. 28). Then he preaches the gospel to the Gentiles there, witnesses the Holy Spirit falling upon them, baptizes them, and stays with them for several days (v. 48). The important implication in this story is that Peter has accepted Gentiles without requiring them to go through circumcision, because he understands that "God shows no partiality but in every nation anyone who fears him and does what is right is acceptable to him" (Acts 10:34–35). A particularist has become a universalist.

According to the immediately following section (Acts 11:1–18), this incident at Cornelius's house caused some controversy in the church of Jerusalem, in which the circumcised believers (οἱ ἐκ περιτομῆς) criticized Peter's association with the Gentiles (v. 2). Peter had to appear before them and give them a full account of how he had changed his mind on the issue of Gentiles (vv. 5–17). Acts says when the Jewish Christians in Jerusalem heard the account, they became silent and then praised God for giving even the Gentiles the opportunity of repentance that would lead to eternal life (v. 18). This suggests they were theologically persuaded by what Peter told them. This fits very well with Luke's typical redactional tendency to present a harmonious picture of early Christian communities, which makes the account a little suspicious. Plus, even in the narrative world of Acts, it will shortly be made clear that not all the circumcision believers were convinced (cf. Acts 15:1, 5).

Incidentally (or not so incidentally), this marks the end of Peter's tenure at the Jerusalem church in Acts. According to Acts 12:1–17, he was subsequently arrested by Herod, put in prison, and then miraculously set free. He next went to the Jerusalem church, but, interestingly enough, he did not enter it. Instead, he said to the maid who answered the door, "Tell this to James and to the believers"—and then he left for another place (v. 17). Again, incidentally (or not so incidentally), this is where James "the Lord's brother" appears in Acts for the first time. Does it indicate that the change of leadership in the Jerusalem church from Peter to James takes place at this point? In any case, Peter would briefly come back later to the Jerusalem church for the Apostolic Council—yet as far as leadership in the Jerusalem church is concerned, he seems to have lost his footing there. One cannot help wondering if Peter's departure was due to his recent "conversion" from particularism to universalism. Perhaps his newly embraced theological stance was not acceptable at the Jerusalem church, which was becoming increasingly particularistic with the strong presence of the circumcision party (οἱ ἐκ περιτομῆς).

As we noted above, Peter's departure happened simultaneously with the ascendancy of James "the Lord's brother" to the leadership position at the Jerusalem church. One may have caused the other, although the connection between the two is only implicit in Acts.[43] It appears that the theological outlook of the Jerusalem church changed as the makeup of the congregation and the leadership changed. First, when the Hellenists were persecuted and eventually left Jerusalem, the Jerusalem church was left with the Hebrews, who were more conservative and more scrupulous about observing the written regulations of the Torah. Then, as James "the Lord's brother," who had never been a disciple of Jesus in his Galilean ministry, took over the leadership after Peter's departure, the church became more rigid and particularistic, especially on the question of the acceptance of the uncircumcised Gentiles (Acts 15:1, 5).

Chapter 3

The Apostolic Council
in Jerusalem

ESTABLISHMENT OF THE ANTIOCH CHURCH

According to Acts 11:19, those Hellenists[1] who had left Jerusalem because of the persecution traveled to Phoenicia, Cyprus, and Antioch, where they preached the word *to no one except Jews* (εἰ μὴ μόνον Ἰουδαίοις).[2] That is, even the Hellenists from the Jerusalem church were not interested in Gentile mission. The theological implication is that in the mind of the earliest Jewish Christians in Jerusalem salvation was believed to be reserved for the covenant people—that is, the Torah-observant Jews.[3]

Whether Second Temple Judaism was a missionary religion is still a matter of debate, which goes beyond the scope of this book.[4] If Judaism in the first century C.E. in general did not engage in active Gentile mission, there is nothing unusual about the Hellenists preaching to Jews only (Acts 11:19). If, on the other hand, there were active missionary activities toward Gentiles in Second Temple Judaism, the Jewish Christians in Acts—both the Hebrews and the Hellenists—can be said to belong to the more particularist end of the spectrum within Judaism with regard to their soteriology.

Put in that context, Acts 11:20 presents a turning point in the history of early Christian mission: those who went to Antioch preached also to the Gentiles,[5] and a great number of the Gentiles became believers, apparently without being circumcised. In Acts this marks the first instance that a Jewish Christian church engages in Gentile mission with the result that Gentiles qua Gentiles join the church, even though it was only at the beginning stage of the establishment of the church.[6] The author of Acts highlights the significance of this mission by saying that it was in Antioch that believers were first called Christians (Χριστιανοί, Acts 11:26). The term Χριστιανοί refers to a group of people who share a common belief in Christ. As such it does not designate an ethnic group but a socioreligious community.[7] This highly redactional statement of Luke shows his notion of what a Christian church should ultimately be doing in their mission: that is, preaching the gospel to the world without making a distinction between Jews and Gentiles. Even though this account seems to have been overshadowed by Luke's theological concerns, there is no compelling reason to doubt its historical core.[8] With this breakthrough in mission practice, the Antioch church was soon to be the center of Gentile mission in early Christianity.

According to Acts 11:22, the news of this successful Gentile mission by the Antioch church reached Jerusalem and the Jerusalem church sent Barnabas to Antioch.[9] (Barnabas's presence at the church in Antioch is also attested by Gal. 2:11–14.) The news must have alarmed the particularists in the Jerusalem church. They may have wanted to monitor the situation of the newly formed Antioch church so that they might eventually be able to persuade the Gentile converts to receive circumcision and to observe the Torah commandments. If that is the reason the Jerusalem church sent Barnabas, their original plan did not work, because Barnabas ended up endorsing the Gentile mission without circumcision in the Antioch church and became one of their leaders.

According to Acts 11:25–26, one of the first things that Barnabas did in Antioch was to go to Tarsus and bring Saul to the Antioch church as his coworker. This account coheres with Paul's own recollection in Galatians 1:20, in which he mentions Cilicia as the last place of his mission before his ministry in Antioch, even though he does not say he was brought to Antioch by Barnabas.[10] Acts reports a great success of the ministry of Barnabas and Paul in Antioch with the implication that they brought many Gentiles to the church without having them circumcised. If that was the case, the Antioch church was incubating a potentially serious conflict with the Jerusalem church over the relation between Jews and Gentiles in the same community.

THE APOSTOLIC COUNCIL IN JERUSALEM

Regardless of how much is historical and how much is legendary in the stories of Paul's so-called first missionary journey in Acts 13:1–14:28, what is certain is that Paul and Barnabas were actively engaged in Gentile mission both in Antioch and in the surrounding regions.[11] As a result, an increasing number of uncircumcised Gentiles seems to have joined the Antioch church. According to Acts 15:1, certain individuals came to Antioch from Judea[12] and said to the Gentile members of the church, "Unless you are circumcised according to the custom of Moses, you cannot be saved."[13] This statement clearly represents a more exclusive soteriology, according to which salvation is only for the covenant people (that is, the Torah-observant Jews). Other people may be saved but only when they become Jews— in the case of males, by going through both circumcision and proselyte baptism, and in the case of females, by going through the latter only.[14] In the diversity of the belief system of Second Temple Judaism, this ethnocentric/particularistic soteriology would certainly not have been held by every Jew, but it may not have been a negligible minority opinion among the Jews, either. In any case, the individuals who came down to Antioch from Judea acted according to their theological conviction of particularism, which was at odds with the universalism that provided the theological foundation of the Gentile mission of Paul and Barnabas in the Antioch church.[15]

As a result, a serious controversy seems to have arisen in the Antioch church over the issue of how Gentiles could be saved (Acts 15:2). The sheer fact that the members of the Antioch church could not simply ignore the claim of the particularists from Judea may indicate that there was a higher and uncontestable authority behind them, for which the Jerusalem church with James the Lord's brother as its leader would be the most reasonable candidate. Most probably, that is why the issue was finally brought up to the Jerusalem church, which resulted in the so-called first Apostolic Council in the Jerusalem church.[16]

Fixing the date for the Apostolic Council in Jerusalem is impossible. According to Paul's autobiographical account in Galatians 1:13–2:14, the trip to Jerusalem for the Apostolic Council is his second visit to Jerusalem after his conversion. He says he went to Jerusalem "after fourteen years" (Gal. 2:1). It is not clear whether or not this reference to "fourteen years" is inclusive of the "three years" mentioned in Galatians 1:18 with regard to Paul's first visit to Jerusalem after his conversion. However, since the date of his conversion can only be estimated backward from later points of reference, such as the Gallio inscription or the proconsulship of Festus, this question does not affect the date for the Apostolic Council in Jerusalem. If the Apostolic Council in Jerusalem preceded the Antioch Incident and Paul's first stay in Corinth (51–53 C.E.), as I believe it did, the council must have happened sometime during 48–49 C.E., which would allow an adequate amount of time for Paul's missionary activities in Macedonia prior to his coming to Corinth.[17]

There are two accounts of the Apostolic Council in Jerusalem in the New Testament: Acts 15:1–35 and Galatians 2:1–10. In spite of doubts raised by some scholars because of their discrepancies, the two accounts do seem to refer to the same event.[18] Even though the primary account of Paul in Galatians 2 should have priority, as historical data neither Acts 15 nor Galatians 2 should be taken at face value. The former is secondary and tendentious in nature, and the latter was written in a highly apologetic and polemical context.[19] There is enough common ground between the two, however, that a certain historical core can be reconstructed. Both accounts agree that the issue was whether Gentile converts should be circumcised in order to be saved. As Acts 15:5 indicates, the requirement of circumcision was not just an isolated requisite but a symbol of the membership of the covenant people and the obligation to observe the commandments of the Torah in its entirety.

Paul's statement in Galatians 2:2 (μή πως εἰς κενὸν τρέχω ἢ ἔδραμον) indicates that he thought the result of this meeting would have a decisive impact on the future of his mission. Apparently, endorsement by the Jerusalem church was very important for anybody who wanted to preach the gospel, and Paul seems to be conscious of that.[20] Also, on the theological side, the issue was how Gentiles could be saved—and the decisions of this council would have immediate implications for the question of the salvific efficacy of the Torah, which was a crucial question for Paul. So, for him, the issue on the table of the Apostolic Council in Jerusalem concerned the fundamental principle of his soteriology, and therefore the very "truth of the gospel" (ἡ ἀλήθεια τοῦ εὐαγγελίου) was at stake (v. 5). It was Paul's belief that, if observation of the commandments of the Torah (including circumcision) was judged to be necessary for Gentiles to be saved, then the redemption of Jesus Christ did not have sufficient salvific efficacy, leaving salvation exclusively for the Torah-abiding Jews as a covenant people. Such a view would seriously undermine Paul's Christology and his universalistic soteriology. Then Paul's mission, which was based on his theology of salvation through the redemption of Jesus Christ for all humans, would turn out to be in vain. That is why he says, "If justification comes through the law, then Christ died for nothing" (Gal. 2:21b).

According to Galatians 2:1–3, Paul and Barnabas were accompanied by the Gentile convert Titus. The circumcision party in Jerusalem, who considered circumcision as a critical requirement for Gentile believers (Acts 15:5), tried unsuccessfully to force him to be circumcised (οὐδὲ Τίτος ... Ἕλλην ὤν, ἠναγκάσθη περιτμηθῆναι).[21] Apparently, both parties regarded Titus's case as a symbolic representation of the theological issue at stake even before the meeting was convened.[22] Under the auspices of Paul and Barnabas, Titus managed to resist the pressure for circumcision from the particularist faction in Jerusalem (Gal. 2:5).[23]

What actually took place at the Apostolic Council meeting at the Jerusalem church is difficult to reconstruct. In Galatians 2:1–10, Paul seems to imply that the Antioch delegates had two separate meetings at the Jerusalem church: one with the whole church and the other with the "pillars" of the church only.[24] The details of these separate meetings are not narrated by Paul, but, regardless of the exact proceedings, it is clear from his report that the critical decision was made by the key leaders, including James.[25] In contrast, the account of the Apostolic Council in Acts 15 reports only one formal plenary meeting. In that account, James sits as chair, with the Pharisaic believers from Jerusalem on the one side of the table and the delegates from Antioch on the other, each advocating one of the two opposing soteriological views.[26] Then Peter, as the representative apostle, gives a speech in support of the position of the delegates of the Antioch church (Acts 15:7–11).[27] At the conclusion of the meeting, James as the chair summarizes the arguments and makes the final deliberation (vv. 13–21), which sanctions the Gentile mission without circumcision. Then the "apostles and presbyters" (v. 22, my translation) send delegations to the Gentile believers in Antioch, Syria, and Cilicia with an encyclical (vv. 13–21), which is commonly called the Apostolic Decree. This decree is not mentioned by Paul. This omission, coupled with the fact that the decree's content differs from what Paul says in Galatians 2:1–10 about the decisions made at the meeting, raises a serious question with regard to its historicity.[28]

The critical problem lies in the four additional stipulations at the end of the Apostolic Decree, which Paul does not seem to be aware of. They are prohibitions from idol meat, blood, what is strangled, and fornication (Acts 15:29). It is possible that Paul intentionally omitted this decree in his report of the meeting to the Galatians. However, since he says, "They added nothing to me" (Gal. 2:6, my translation), it is more plausible that there were no added injunctions at the Apostolic Council in Jerusalem. Moreover, if Paul had known of such stipulations, he would have referred to them in 1 Corinthians 8 and Romans 14, in which he discusses the question of eating idol meat. So, this set of additional stipulations seems to be a Lukan composition patterned after the Noahide Law for the Gentiles.

In contrast to Luke's account of the additional "requirements" for the Gentiles, Paul himself says that the Jerusalem leaders requested the Antioch delegates to remember the poor in Jerusalem, to which he gladly assented (Gal. 2:10). This would naturally be seen as a visible sign of the unity of the church, which the Apostolic Council had just affirmed by sanctioning the two gospels. At least, that is how Paul saw it, and this would become an important factor in the last phase of his life, to which I will come back in Chapter 6.

On the surface, the final decision of the Apostolic Council in Jerusalem looks like a one-sided triumph of the Antioch delegation, but a close reading of Paul's report reveals that it was a concession by both parties in the sense that two different gospels were recognized there: *the gospel of the circumcision* (τὸ εὐαγγέλιον τῆς περιτομῆς) and *the gospel of the uncircumcision* (τὸ εὐαγγέλιον τῆς ἀκροβυστίας, Gal. 2:7).[29] These two gospels represented two different soteriologies as well as two different mission fields: Peter was given the apostolate of the circumcision (ἀποστολὴν τῆς περιτομῆς)[30] and Paul was sent to the Gentiles (εἰς τὰ ἔθνη, Gal. 2:8).[31] In other words, the Jerusalem particularists yielded to the Antioch universalists and recognized their gospel of the uncircumcision as legitimate, and by the same token the latter also yielded to the former and recognized their gospel of the circumcision as legitimate. Theological differences were resolved by mutual recognition.[32] Also, the conciliatory attitude of James toward Paul, at least at the Apostolic Council in Acts 15, might even be historical, even though the whole picture fits rather well with Luke's redactional tendency toward harmonization in early Christianity. In that sense the Apostolic Council in Jerusalem represents the spirit of unity of the church at its best.[33] The course of the history of Christianity in the next two millennia would have been very different had both parties continued to honor the concession according to this spirit of unity.

THE ANTIOCH INCIDENT

Paul, Barnabas, and Titus came back from the Apostolic Council in Jerusalem to the Antioch church with their gospel of the uncircumcision fully sanctioned by the Jerusalem authorities. Titus, who was pressured to be circumcised by the particularist party in the Jerusalem church, came back uncircumcised and subsequently became a living symbol of the fully recognized validity of the gospel of the uncircumcision (Gal. 2:3). Now, the Antioch church was to become the de jure as well as de facto center of the circumcision-free Gentile mission based on universalism. Shortly after their return from Jerusalem, however, an unfortunate confrontation took place in the Antioch church that had to do with the relation between Jews and Gentiles.

In terms of the sequence of events in Paul's autobiographical section in Galatians, the Antioch Incident (2:11–14) immediately follows the Apostolic Council in Jerusalem (vv. 1–10), which means at least that is how Paul remembered and related the chronological order between them. It is true that a sequence of events in a text does not necessarily mean their chronological order. That is the case with ancient rhetoric as well. In fact, Quintilian expressly allows flexibility with regard to arranging the events when composing the *narratio* section of an oration.[34] However, under normal circumstances, chronological order should be assumed unless there is enough implication in the text to suspect otherwise. In the case of the *narratio* section of Galatians (1:11–2:14), Paul is consistently chronological in his presentation of his life events from the beginning up to this point (1:11–24), and there is no reason why he would reverse the order for the last two events (2:1–14). So, even though there is debate among scholars concerning this issue, I follow the majority opinion, which accepts the order of Galatians 2:1–14.[35]

The order between the Apostolic Council in Jerusalem and the Antioch Incident is important here, because it shows how the agreement reached at the Apostolic Council in Jerusalem was actually honored (or not) by both parties in its immediate aftermath. Perhaps the decision of the Apostolic Council was so theologically loaded that there were enough ambiguities for conflicting interpretations.[36] Pauline chronology based on the "Gallio inscription"[37] and the reference to "fourteen years" in Galatians 2:1 indicates that the time gap between the Apostolic Council in Jerusalem and the Antioch Incident is very small.[38] That is, the Antioch Incident happened when the memory of the Apostolic Council in Jerusalem was still fresh. Moreover, the two events are closely related not only historically but also theologically, as is indicated by Paul's use of the same phrase, ἡ ἀλήθεια τοῦ εὐαγγελίου, to characterize what the two events are about (vv. 5, 14). From this, it is clear that for Paul nothing less than *the truth of the gospel* was at stake in both cases.

The course of events began with a visit of Peter to the Antioch church soon after the Apostolic Council in Jerusalem (Gal. 2:11). It is not known why he came to Antioch or for how long he intended to stay. It is reasonable to conjecture that he might have wanted the Antioch church to be the basis of his future mission, however, since he had lost his leadership position at the Jerusalem church to James. If there is any historicity in Luke's accounts of Peter's "conversion" in Acts 10 and if the Lukan composition of Peter's speech in Acts 15:7–11 expresses a "general sense" (ξυμπᾶσα γνώμη)[39] of what the historical Peter would have said, it is understandable why he would want to go to Antioch and work with Paul and Barnabas: he had become theologically close to them with regard to the terms of inclusion of Gentiles. Peter's joining Paul and Barnabas in Antioch would not be against the agreement of the Apostolic Council in Jerusalem (Gal. 2:8), which only distinguished the two missions in terms of target audience, not according to geographical division.

Apparently, the Jews and the uncircumcised Gentiles at the Antioch church shared common table fellowship, especially for the Lord's Supper, which was most likely an integral part of their worship.[40] Obviously, the ethos of the Torah-free mission, which served as the basis for the abolishment of the requirement of circumcision for Gentile converts, inspired the Jewish members of the Antioch church to have table fellowship with the uncircumcised Gentile believers, even though this would have been seen by many Jews at that time as breaking the purity law (cf. Acts 10:28).[41] Now, Galatians 2:12 says when Peter came to Antioch he ate with the Gentile believers, which means that he willingly followed the practice of the Antioch church and participated in the common table with the Gentiles, either as a guest or as a newly arrived leader. Such behavior is perfectly understandable in light of Acts 10, in which Peter had already broken the purity law and eaten with the Gentiles because of his new understanding of God's dealing with Gentiles. Peter's visit to the mixed congregation in Antioch and his participation in their common meal must have been viewed as a sign of the unity between the gospel of the circumcision represented by Peter and the gospel of the uncircumcision represented by Paul and Barnabas, the quintessential ethos of the decision of the Apostolic Council in Jerusalem.

Unfortunately, this happy mood of unity between Jews and Gentiles in the Antioch church was soon to be shattered, when "certain individuals from James" (τινας ἀπὸ Ἰακώβου, Gal. 2:12) came to intervene.[42] The proper noun Ἰάκωβος in this verse is an unmistakable reference to James the Lord's brother in the Jerusalem church. This is a critical piece of information about the provenance of the legalistic intruders at the Antioch church. They are the delegates of James the Lord's brother, and as such they represent the theological stance of James, in whose authority they acted the way they did. It does not matter whether they were actually sent by James or came of their own will. What matters is that they represented the authority of James in the theological position that they advocated.[43] Paul identifies them as the "circumcision faction" (τοὺς ἐκ περιτομῆς) in the same verse (v. 12). In other words, this group implicitly advocated the theological premise that the observation of the commandments of the Torah, especially circumcision, is a sine qua non for salvation.

Paul's description of Peter's change of behavior in Galatians 2:12 makes it clear that these people from the circumcision faction of the Jerusalem church accused the Jewish members of the Antioch church of breaking the purity law by having table fellowship with uncircumcised Gentiles. Apparently, they also demanded that all the Jews in the Antioch church be immediately withdrawn from the common table with the Gentiles. Technically speaking, these individuals from James do not seem to have infringed the agreement of the Apostolic Council in Jerusalem per se by demanding the Jews to separate themselves from the Gentiles.

However, their demand shows that they neither understood nor honored the *theological* foundation for the agreement of the Apostolic Council in Jerusalem, which was also at the very core of Paul's universalistic soteriology: that God's new universal salvation transcends ethnic boundaries.[44] They may not have broken the *letter* of the agreement, but they certainly broke the *spirit* of the decision of the Apostolic Council in Jerusalem. It is in that sense that these individuals from James should be regarded as opponents of Paul.[45]

Obviously, the intruders' demand for separation was instantly effective, probably because of the weight of the Jamesian authority that they represented. First, Peter withdrew from the table fellowship with the Gentile believers "for fear of those from the circumcision faction," according to Paul's observation (Gal. 2:12, my translation). Then, the rest of the Jewish believers, including even Barnabas, followed suit. Paul alone among the leaders of the Antioch church remained undeterred. Paul judged the behavior of his fellow Jewish leaders as hypocritical (Gal. 2:13) in the sense that they failed to act in accordance with their theological conviction that God does not differentiate Jews and Gentiles with regard to salvation.[46] In Paul's mind, what Peter, Barnabas, and other Jewish believers belied by their withdrawal from the common table with the Gentile believers was no less than *the truth of the gospel* (ἡ ἀλήθεια τοῦ εὐαγγελίου, Gal. 2:14a), according to which there should be no soteriologically binding distinction between Jews and Gentiles in Christ. So Paul confronted Peter before all and said, "If you, though a Jew, live like a Gentile and not like a Jew, how can you compel the Gentiles to live like Jews?" (Gal. 2:14b).

This statement of Paul may suggest that more was at stake in the demand of the Jerusalem delegates than just advising the Jewish believers to refrain from table fellowship with the Gentile believers. The phrase τὰ ἔθνη ἀναγκάζεις ἰουδαΐζειν implies that the delegates from James, implicitly or explicitly, forced the Gentile believers in Antioch to "Judaize" (ἰουδαΐζειν), which would mean to conform to the Jewish religious practices, especially the observation of the commandments of the Torah.[47] If that is the case, their demand amounts to virtual rejection of the theological principle of the agreement of the Apostolic Council in Jerusalem as Paul interpreted it, and that is why he was so furious that Peter and Barnabas complied with the demand. Paul's account of the Antioch Incident in Galatians 2:11–14 seamlessly flows right into the *thematic* section (vv. 15–21) of the letter,[48] as if Galatians 2:11–21 forms one literary unit. That means Paul regards the issue of the Antioch Incident as a critical one relating to the very heart of the gospel he knew and preached (v. 16). It is in that sense that Paul regarded the Antioch Incident and the Galatian Incident as being of the same kind. Both were about the truth of the gospel as he knew it.

Since Paul does not tell us what the results of the Antioch Incident were, we can only make a reasoned guess about its immediate aftermath. First of all, Paul does not say who prevailed at the incident, which is a strong indication that he is the one who lost out.[49] Also, it seems that Paul eventually lost his footing in the Antioch church as a result of the incident. Apart from this passage (Gal. 2:11), Paul never mentions the name "Antioch" again in any of his letters.[50] There is no indication that Paul maintained good relationship with the Antioch church after this incident.

It is remarkable that Luke is completely silent about the Antioch Incident in Acts. It is possible that he did not know about it at all or that he knew about it but chose not to tell it for some unknown reason. Either way, Luke's failure to narrate the Antioch Incident in Acts creates a serious shortcoming in his presentation of the history of Paul's mission, because it was one of the most important events in Paul's life. Acts does have a brief reference to what must have been the result of the Antioch Incident.[51] That is, immediately after the account of the Apostolic Council in Jerusalem, which is where the Antioch Incident ought to have been narrated, Acts has a short report of a conflict between Barnabas and Paul, which eventually caused them to part company with each other (15:36–41). Acts says the split was the result of a dispute over the issue of whether or not to take along John Mark for their next missionary journey (vv. 37–38). That particular issue might have been an immediate triggering factor, but from Galatians 2:11–14 we already know that there was a more serious conflict between them that must have been the root cause of their eventual split.

Incidentally, it is interesting to notice here that according to Luke's account it is Barnabas and Mark, not Paul and Silas, who seem to have taken up the originally planned missionary route after the split. Acts 15:36 says that the purpose of the intended "second" missionary journey of Barnabas and Paul was to visit the cities in which they had done missionary work in their "first" missionary journey together. So it is likely that they would have traveled the same route as their previous one, which began with their visit to Cyprus (Acts 13:4). According to Acts 15:39, after the split Barnabas and Mark went to Cyprus, while Paul and Silas had to go elsewhere. This means that Paul and Silas had to pioneer new places for their missionary work. The practical implication is that Barnabas and John Mark remained as official missionaries of the Antioch church, whereas Paul and Silas were left on their own.

It may not be a coincidence that Acts now mentions for the first time Paul's manual labor in support of his own ministry during his "second" missionary journey (Acts 18:3), which took place immediately after the split. In other words, it is probably from this point on that Paul had to do "tent-making ministry" to support himself, because he could no longer rely on the financial support from the Antioch church, which probably went to Barnabas and John Mark.

From this point to the end, Acts makes no mention of the Antioch church except for a passing remark on Paul's short visit to Antioch after his "second missionary journey" (Acts 18:22).[52] This makes a strong impression that even in the narrative world of Acts, in which historical accounts are often skewed by Luke's ideal picture of early Christianity, the breach between Paul and the Antioch church was not easily mended. The theological implication of the Antioch Incident was so great that its impact turned out to be long-lasting. One could even say that the Antioch Incident shaped the course of Paul's missionary work for the next ten or so years, during which time all his known epistles were written.[53]

The aftermath of the Antioch Incident, as we have conjectured it, is somewhat surprising. At the contentious moment of the Antioch Incident, Paul seems to be the only one who acted with integrity: Peter and Barnabas behaved hypocritically, at least according to Paul's own reconstruction of the event in Galatians 2:11–14. It is true that these verses were written in a highly polemical context and that we do not have another version of the same story told from the viewpoint of Peter, Barnabas, or James—but it is equally true that precisely because Paul wrote the passage in a polemical context, he could not afford to distort basic facts. In any case, the Antioch Incident is another indication that James the Lord's brother had firmly established himself as the uncontested leader of the Jerusalem church by that time, and as such he wielded enormous influence on other early Christian communities.

EXCURSUS: THE ANTIOCH CHURCH
AFTER THE INCIDENT

The history of early Christian communities in Antioch between the Antioch Incident and the period of Ignatius of Antioch is not known to us. However, if the widely accepted scholarly opinion is correct that Antioch in Syria is the provenience of the Gospel of Matthew,[54] which was probably written sometime in the last decades of the first century, we know that Antioch continued to play an important role in early Christianity after Paul's tenure there. The fact that the Petrine tradition in the Gospel of Matthew is the strongest of all the canonical Gospels (cf. Matt. 16:17–19) may indicate that Peter stayed on in Antioch for some time after the Antioch Incident, leaving his legacy there—which later crystallized into the Gospel of Matthew.[55]

Also, the final redactor of the Gospel of Matthew has a strong theological tendency to advocate universalism over against the particularism firmly held by some members of the Matthean community (cf. Matt. 10:5–6; 15:24). That may reflect one phase of the history of the Antioch church—that is, from 50 to 80 C.E.—in which the church was leaning toward a more conservative soteriology with particularism as a defining term.[56] This may have been the result of the influence of James, as was the case with the Antioch Incident. If so, then Matthew must have been a theologian of the community who tried to redirect its theological leanings toward universalism, advocating active Gentile mission and at the same time preserving the essence of the Jewish heritage.[57] It is important to note that the theology of Ignatius of Antioch, who is the first known church father to quote passages from the Gospel of Matthew, is manifestly Pauline. The strong Pauline character of Ignatius of Antioch implies that Matthew's Gospel was successful in implementing universalism in his community, which would eventually lead the community away from their particularistic past and toward the universalism of the emerging ecumenical church, which was a largely Gentile phenomenon by the early second century.

Chapter 4

Paul's Corinthian Stay
and the Galatian Incident

PAUL'S WORK IN GALATIA AND MACEDONIA

The Antioch Incident forced Paul to become a missionary independent of the Antioch church, which had been the basis of both his residential and itinerant mission for an extended period of time, even though we do not know exactly how long. The so-called second missionary journey in Acts falls into this post-Antioch period of Paul's career as an independent missionary. Again, the historicity of this missionary journey has been questioned, but, apart from legendary materials, the basic outline of Paul's itinerary is to be taken as historical.

Acts 15:41–16:1 mentions Syria, Cilicia, Derbe, and Lystra as the places Paul and Silas went through first. Then Acts 16:6 has a strange expression: "having been forbidden by the Holy Spirit (κωλυθέντες ὑπὸ τοῦ ἁγίου πνεύματος) to speak the word in Asia." The following verse also has a similar expression: "They attempted to go into Bithynia, but the Spirit of Jesus did not allow them" (οὐκ εἴασεν αὐτοὺς τὸ πνεῦμα Ἰησοῦ). Even though it is not clear what Luke means by these verses, they seem to reflect the actual difficulties Paul and Silas may have faced as freelance missionaries without support from the Antioch church or the Jerusalem church. If Paul indeed went through Galatia, as Acts 16:6 says he did, it is probable that he founded the Galatian church at that time,[1] although no definitive conclusion could be drawn on this issue.[2] If the founding of the church happened then, the allusions in Acts 16:6–7 to the difficulties of Paul during that time fit rather well with Paul's own recollection of his predicaments at the time of his founding the Galatian church (Gal. 4:13–14).[3] According to Paul, the members of the church received him "as a messenger (ἄγγελος) of God" as they received Christ Jesus (v. 14), in spite of his weakness (ἀσθένεια). The term ἄγγελος is ambiguous. It can mean an angelic being or a human messenger of God.[4] Here I take it to mean a *messenger* who delivers the *message* (εὐαγγέλιον) of salvation. The message is, of course, the gospel of salvation by the grace of God through the faith/faithfulness in/of Jesus Christ[5] apart from the works of the law (2:16). This gospel is the same gospel of the uncircumcision endorsed by the Apostolic Council in Jerusalem (v. 7), and it does not require the Gentile believers to become like Jews. The churches of Galatia were founded on this universalistic soteriology of the gospel of the uncircumcision.

It seems that the next significant locus of Paul's ministry after his stay in Galatia is Macedonia. From the existing letters of Paul we know there were Pauline churches in the two leading Macedonian cities, Philippi and Thessalonica. Paul would have founded these Macedonian churches soon after he crossed over the Aegean Sea—moving westward, as he implies he did (Rom. 15:19). Pauline chronology does not allow us to assign a long period for Paul's stay in either city. Several months in each case would have been maximum.[6]

It is to be assumed that Paul continued to preach the same gospel as he had started with—that is, the gospel of salvation by grace through the faith/faithfulness in/of Jesus Christ apart from the works of the Torah—which was once dubbed "the gospel of the uncircumcision" (τὸ εὐαγγέλιον τῆς ἀκρο-βυστίας, Gal. 2:7). Indeed, Philippians 3:9 ("not having a righteousness of my own that comes from the law, but one that comes through faith in Christ, the righteousness from God based on faith")—which is a personalized version of the gospel of the uncircumcision expressed in the first person singular form—may let us safely assume that Paul preached the same gospel to the Philippians as he did to the Galatians. Acts 16:16–40 tells a story of the imprisonment of Paul and Silas in Philippi, of which the details beg questions of historicity. It is probable that Paul himself is referring to the same hardship, however, when he says in 1 Thessalonians 2:2, "Though we had already suffered and been shamefully mistreated at Philippi, as you know, we had courage in our God to declare to you the gospel of God in spite of great opposition."[7] This suffering may have caused Paul and Silas to leave Philippi and go to the neighboring major city, Thessalonica.

Paul says in 1 Thessalonians 2:2 that, in spite of the great opposition, he and Silas were undaunted and came to the Thessalonians with the courage to proclaim "the gospel of God" (τὸ εὐαγγέλιον τοῦ θεοῦ), which is another reference to the same gospel that Paul always preached (that is, the gospel of the uncircumcision). He also says in 1 Thessalonians 2:9 that he and Silas worked night and day in order not to burden the Thessalonian believers. Apparently, Paul and Silas had to provide for themselves because they could no longer depend on financial support from the Antioch church. The suffering inflicted on Paul and Silas by "the Jews" (οἱ Ἰουδαῖοι, Acts 17:5) in Thessalonica, which is narrated in Acts 17:5–9, does not have a clear cross reference in Paul's letters, but 1 Thessalonians 2:17 does seem to refer to an undesirable situation that eventually caused Paul and Silas to leave Thessalonica rather abruptly. Thus the short period of Paul's Macedonian ministry came to a premature ending.

THE CORINTHIAN PERIOD
AND THE GALATIAN INCIDENT

The Beginning of Paul's Ministry in Corinth

The itinerary of Paul from Thessalonica to Corinth is not clear. There is an extensive account in Acts about Paul's missionary activities in Beroea (Acts 17:10–15) and Athens (vv. 16–34). Paul himself never mentions Beroea but he does talk about his stay in Athens after his departure from Thessalonica (1 Thess. 3:1). Given the tendency of Paul to gravitate to large urban areas for his mission,[8] it is only natural that he visited Athens, the cultural capital of the Mediterranean world, and made an effort to proclaim the gospel there.[9] The Areopagus speech (Acts 17:22–31), which is largely a Lukan composition, should not be taken to reproduce the actual missionary speech Paul putatively preached there. If I may borrow the language of Thucydides, though, it may contain what Luke thinks is the "general sense" (ἡ ξυμπᾶσα γνώμη) of what Paul would have said in such an occasion.[10]

Whatever the results of Paul's work at Athens might have been, he did not stay there long and he probably did not establish a church there. Instead, he moved down southwest to Corinth and settled there. For the first time since his departure from Antioch, Paul ended up staying in one place for an extended period of time. Acts 18:2 says that in Corinth Paul met Aquila and Priscilla, the Jewish couple who had left Rome because of the edict of Claudius. This edict of Claudius is mentioned by Suetonius[11] and dated by Orosius as "his ninth year," that is, ca. 49 C.E.[12] Together with the Gallio inscription (cf. Acts 18:12–17), which dates his proconsulship from 51–52 C.E., this would put Paul's stay in Corinth from late 49/early 50 to mid-51/late 51 C.E.[13]

Acts 18:3 says Paul stayed with Aquila and Priscilla because they were of the same trade (ὁμότεχνοι), that is, tentmakers (σκηνοποιοί). Paul mentions their names in 1 Corinthians 16:19 and Romans 16:3–4, both of which are related with the Corinthian church in one way or another. In the former, Priscilla and Aquila are quoted as sending greetings to the Corinthians from the church in their house in Asia (probably in Ephesus). In the latter, they are among the intended addressees of Paul's greetings in the church of Rome. Romans 16:5a also indicates that the couple is hosting a house church in their home in Rome. These references in Paul's letters indicate that Priscilla and Aquila worked with Paul in Corinth and subsequently in Ephesus. Then, if Romans 16 is part of the original text of Romans, which is still debated, the couple eventually went back to Rome and joined the believers there. This itinerary of Priscilla and Aquila fits with Acts 18:18–19, according to which they accompanied Paul when he left Corinth for Ephesus and stayed on in Ephesus after his departure from there.

Thus, the Pauline church of Corinth probably began at the house of Priscilla and Aquila. Romans 16:4 implies that much of their work was devoted to the mission and ministry for the Gentiles, which tells us what the focus of Paul's ministry was in Corinth and subsequently in Ephesus. Concerning the beginning of his work in Corinth, Paul says,

> When I came to you, brothers and sisters, I did not come proclaiming the mystery of God to you in lofty words or wisdom. For I decided to know nothing among you except Jesus Christ, and him crucified. And I came to you in weakness and in fear and in much trembling. My speech and my proclamation were not with plausible words of wisdom, but with a demonstration of the Spirit and of power, so that your faith might rest not on human wisdom but on the power of God. (1 Cor. 2:1–5)

This reminds us of what he also says about the beginning of his Galatian ministry in Galatians 4:13–14:

> You know that it was because of a physical infirmity that I first announced the gospel to you; though my condition put you to the test, you did not scorn or despise me, but welcomed me as an angel of God, as Christ Jesus.

The time gap between Paul's arrival in Galatia and that in Corinth is probably less than a year. The comparison between 1 Corinthians 2:1–5 and Galatians 4:13–14 tells us that apparently the big picture had not changed. Paul was still in a hostile environment, so he came to Corinth "in weakness, in fear, and in much trembling." The negative force against his mission included, as will be made clear later in this book, the *potential* as well as the *actual* influence of the particularist soteriology that characterized the theological outlook of the Jerusalem church with James as the head.

According to Acts 17:14, while Paul traveled down from Macedonia to Corinth via Athens, Silas and Timothy were left behind in Macedonia with a plan to rejoin Paul later. Then, Acts 18:5 says, Timothy and Silas finally came down from Macedonia to join Paul in Corinth. First Thessalonians 3:1–3, on the other hand, says Timothy was sent by Paul from Athens to the Thessalonian church to strengthen and encourage them, and verse 6 says Timothy came back from Thessalonica to Paul. Whatever the detail of the itinerary of Timothy was, Paul was worrying about the Thessalonian church between his departure and Timothy's return. He says in 1 Thessalonians 3:5,

> For this reason, when I could bear it no longer, I sent to find out about your faith; I was afraid that somehow the tempter had tempted you and that our labor had been *in vain* (εἰς κενόν). (italics added)

The fear of Paul that someone could do something to his church in Thessalonica to the effect that his missionary labor would turn out to be in vain (εἰς κενόν) has a very close parallel in Galatians 2:2, which describes the fear that he had when he was going up to Jerusalem to discuss the issue of the requirement of circumcision for Gentile converts:

I went up in response to a revelation. Then I laid before them (though only in a private meeting with the acknowledged leaders) the gospel that I proclaim among the Gentiles, in order to make sure that I was not running, or had not run, *in vain* (εἰς κενόν). (italics added)

In that regard, it seems reasonable to believe that in both 1 Thessalonians 3:5 and Galatians 2:2 Paul is talking about the same kind of fear that the gospel he preached—that is, the gospel of the uncircumcision—could be nullified by the attack from the particularists, who would enforce the gospel of the circumcision on the newly converted Gentile believers in the Thessalonian church and in the Galatian church. It is not known whether the particularists actually came to the Thessalonian church to demand circumcision. Whatever happened in the Thessalonian church, however, Paul's fear in 1 Thessalonians 3:5 turned out to be unnecessary: Timothy finally came back and delivered to Paul the good news that the Thessalonian believers were standing firm in their faith and love (1 Thess. 3:6). To Paul's great relief, the Thessalonian church had not been affected by the particularists. In response to this good news, Paul wrote a paraenetic letter to them, which was later to be known as 1 Thessalonians, the earliest book in the New Testament.

The Galatian Incident

Unfortunately, this temporary peace in Paul's ministry does not seem to have lasted long. While Paul was working hard to lay the foundation for the Corinthian church and establish it firmly (1 Cor. 3:6, 10), a serious problem was arising in the churches of Galatia. This eventually led to another major trauma in Paul's career as an "apostle" of Christ after the Antioch Incident.[14] I will call it the "Galatian Incident" in this book in order to make it parallel with the Antioch Incident.

As is the case with the latter, Acts is again completely silent about the former. Luke either does not know of the Galatian Incident or deliberately leaves it out because it does not fit with his idealistic picture of early church history. In any case, for the reconstruction of this event, the identity of the intruders, and the nature of their claims, we are totally dependent on what Paul has to say in his apologetic letter to the Galatian believers.

In Paul's opinion, the Galatian Incident was a disaster in the churches of Galatia caused by a systematic attack from certain Judaizing intruders against the apostleship of Paul and the gospel he preached (i.e., the gospel of the uncircumcision). First of all, Galatians 1:6 says the Galatian believers were quickly turning away from the one who called them in the grace (of Christ)[15] to "the other gospel" (ἕτερον εὐαγγέλιον), which is immediately juxtaposed against the "gospel of Christ" (τὸ εὐαγγέλιον τοῦ Χριστοῦ) in the following sentence. From the thesis section of the letter (Gal. 2:15–21) we learn what the content of Paul's gospel is. It is the soteriological principle that a human being is not justified by the works of the Torah but through the faith/faithfulness in/of Jesus Christ. This is what Paul means by "the gospel of Christ." Then the other soteriology, which in Paul's judgment relies on the "works of the Torah," is what he refers to as "the other gospel" (ἕτερον εὐαγγέλιον), which is also called "the gospel of the circumcision" (τὸ εὐαγγέλιον τῆς περιτομῆς) in Galatians 2:7.[16]

From these verses we can infer that there were some intruders in the churches of Galatia, and that they successfully managed to persuade the Galatian believers to reject the "gospel of Christ" Paul preached and turn to the "other gospel," which mandated the observation of the commandments of the Torah, including the circumcision law (Gal. 6:12–13) and the ceremonial laws (4:10). The exact identity of these people is unknown, although it is very likely that they had some connection with the Jerusalem church.[17] Paul refers to them as "those who disturb you and wish to pervert the gospel of Christ" (οἱ ταράσσοντες ὑμᾶς καὶ θέλοντες μεταστρέψαι τὸ εὐαγγέλιον τοῦ Χριστοῦ, Gal. 1:7) and "those who perturb you" (οἱ ἀναστατοῦντες ὑμᾶς, Gal. 5:12).

There is even a reference to a single person with a definite article: "the one who is disturbing you" (ὁ ταράσσων ὑμᾶς, Gal. 5:10). This implies that there is a highly recognizable leader in or behind the group of intruders in the churches of Galatia. The identity of this leader is veiled here. The definite article in this phrase indicates that the person referred to is well known to both Paul and his addressees and therefore does not have to be named. It is possible to take this phrase as a reference to a particular ringleader of the Judaizing intruders in the Galatian church. It is also possible to interpret it as an elliptical allusion to *the* authority behind the Judaizing intruders, however—that is, James the Lord's brother of the Jerusalem church.

These intruders also seem to have repudiated Paul's apostolic claim, arguing that he was not qualified to be an apostle because he had never been approved by the Jerusalem authorities as one (Gal. 1:10–12). According to Acts 1:21–22, one of the qualifications for an apostle was that he (*sic*)[18] must have been an eyewitness for the ministry of Jesus from his baptism to his resurrection,[19] and obviously Paul does not meet this requirement. Even though the historical veracity of this Lukan account of the twelve apostles can be debated, a similar identification in the other Synoptic Gospels of the Twelve as apostles indicates the notion was widely, if not unanimously, held in early Christianity that there were only a limited number of people who could be called apostles based on their special relations with Jesus.[20]

The majority of the Galatian believers were easily persuaded by the Judaizing intruders, who denied Paul's gospel and his apostleship on the basis of this widely held notion. Thus they adopted the gospel that the intruders imposed on them, and they began to be circumcised (Gal. 5:2) and to observe the ceremonial laws as prescribed in the Torah (4:10–11). Also, they turned away from Paul, having been persuaded that he was not a legitimate apostle (v. 16). When Paul heard this news in Corinth, he was angry with the Galatian Christians and immediately tried to win them back by writing a letter to the churches of Galatia in defense of his gospel and his apostleship. We now know that letter as Galatians.[21]

The very first sentence of the greeting section of the letter ("Paul an apostle—sent neither by human commission nor from human authorities, but through

Jesus Christ and God the Father, who raised him from the dead," Gal. 1:1) is, in fact, Paul's defense speech on his apostleship, which will be further elaborated in Galatians 1:10–24. Moreover, his first comment on the Galatian apostasy (Gal. 1:6–7) categorically denies the validity of what he dubs the "other gospel" (ἕτερον εὐαγγέλιον):

> I am astounded that you are so quickly turned away from the one who called you in the grace of Christ to the other gospel—not that there is another gospel, but there are some who are confusing you and wishing to pervert the gospel of Christ. (translation mine)

The Greek word ἕτερος, which Paul uses in verse 6 for the phrase ἕτερον εὐαγγέλιον, is a dual pronominal adjective, and its precise meaning is "the other of the two"—in contrast to ἄλλος, which is a more general adjective for "other."[22] So, what Paul means by the phrase ἕτερον εὐαγγέλιον is not just any other gospel but the gospel *other than* the one he preached. At this point it should be remembered that, according to Paul's own accounts in Galatians 2:7, the concession reached at the Apostolic Council in Jerusalem sanctioned these two different gospels as equally legitimate. Now, Paul seems to interpret the Galatian Incident as an indication that his gospel (the gospel of the uncircumcision) had been virtually rejected by the Judaizing intruders, whatever their origin. Accordingly, he was hard pressed to fight back by rejecting their gospel (that is, the gospel of the circumcision). Paul even goes so far as to say that there is no such thing as another gospel, meaning that the gospel of the circumcision has no validity at all. Thus, the spirit of unity of the Apostolic Council in Jerusalem symbolized by the concession that sanctioned two different gospels has already begun to be shattered.

Even though Paul rhetorically says in Galatians 1:6 he is astounded (θαυμάζειν) that the Galatian believers are so quickly turned to the other gospel, it is not difficult to see why they did so. First of all, as long as the Jesus movement was not yet a separate religion from Judaism, the Hebrew Bible was the only Scripture of authority for Christians, Jewish or Gentile, and it prescribes that the observation of the entire Torah is required of the righteous.[23] Moreover, the circumcision, the Sabbath law, and the purity law—all of which had bearing on Jewish-Gentile relations—were regarded by many as the most important commandments: functioning as the identity markers for the covenant people, for whom alone salvation is reserved.[24] It would have been easy for the Judaizing intruders to persuade the Galatian Gentile believers to follow suit in these regards.

Second, as remarked above, Paul was not adequately qualified to be an apostle in the traditional sense of the word, because he was not an eyewitness of Jesus' ministry (Acts 1:21–22)[25] and also because he was a persecutor of the church before his conversion, as he himself admits (1 Cor. 15:9). For these reasons the Jerusalem church never sanctioned Paul's apostleship—and therefore the Judaizing intruders in Galatia would not have had much trouble in convincing the Galatians that Paul was not really an apostle.

It is interesting in this regard to observe how carefully Paul words his report on the agreements of the Apostolic Council in Jerusalem concerning his status vis-à-vis that of Peter in Galatians 2:7–8:

[7] . . . ὅτι πεπίστευμαι τὸ εὐαγγέλιον τῆς ἀκροβυστίας καθὼς Πέτρος (τὸ εὐαγγέλιον) τῆς περιτομῆς,

[8]ὁ γὰρ ἐνεργήσας Πέτρῳ εἰς ἀποστολὴν τῆς περιτομῆς ἐνήργησεν καὶ ἐμοὶ εἰς τὰ ἔθνη.

In verse 7, in which he talks about the gospel of the circumcision and the gospel of the uncircumcision, the phrase τὸ εὐαγγέλιον is omitted before τῆς περιτομῆς in order to avoid redundancy, but there is no room for confusion or ambiguity in the resulting sentence. The meaning is clear: "I have been entrusted with the gospel of the uncircumcision just as Peter (has been entrusted with the gospel) of the circumcision" (my translation). In contrast, the syntactic structure of verse 8 does not allow the assumption that the word ἀποστολήν is to be understood after ἐμοί. That is, the sentence should *not* be taken to mean: "The one who was at work in Peter for the apostleship of the circumcision was at work also in me for the *apostleship* of the Gentiles." Instead, it simply says, "The one who was at work in Peter for the apostleship of the circumcision was at work also in me for the Gentiles" (my translation). Of course, Paul would very much have loved to use the word ἀποστολήν for himself, but he had to be extremely careful, especially in an apologetic letter like Galatians, not to claim for himself a title that was not officially recognized at the Apostolic Council in Jerusalem and that was being questioned of him at the time of his writing the letter. Thus he seems to have opted for a seemingly ambiguous expression, which is not really ambiguous, if read closely.

One of the important aspects of this letter is that there is a long narrative section (Gal. 1:11–2:14), in which Paul provides an autobiographical account regarding some of the critical events in the communities to which he was connected. This section serves as the historical basis for the theological principle of the letter (2:15–21), which immediately follows it.[26] It is remarkable that within the narrative section Paul has a disproportionately long passage for the cause, proceedings, and results of the Apostolic Council in Jerusalem (vv. 1–10) and for the Antioch Incident (vv. 11–14). Also interesting is the fact that the transition from his account of the Antioch Incident (vv. 11–14) to the thematic section of the letter (vv. 15–21) is almost seamless. I take this as a strong indication that Paul sees a fundamental continuity between what happened to the Antioch church before and after the Apostolic Council in Jerusalem and what is happening to the Galatian church. In Paul's judgment the same theological problem lies behind both: that is, the threat to the *freedom* (ἡ ἐλευθερία, Gal. 2:4) in Christ Jesus and to the *truth* of the gospel (ἡ ἀλήθεια τοῦ εὐαγγελίου, Gal. 2:5), which is the *fides*-based universalistic gospel over against the Torah-bound particularistic gospel.

It seems that Paul's statement in Galatians 2:1–14 contains a number of key phrases that can be regarded as indirect allusions to the Galatian Incident. First of all, Galatians 2:4 contains a reference to the intruders at the Antioch church, that is, the "false brothers" (ψευδαδέλφους), who Paul says were secretly brought in to spy out the freedom (τὴν ἐλευθερίαν) he and the Antiochene believers had in Christ Jesus so that they might enslave them. This statement closely parallels Galatians 1:7, in which Paul describes the intruders in the Galatian church as "those who confuse you (οἱ ταράσσοντες ὑμᾶς) and want to pervert (μεταστρέψαι) the gospel of Christ" (my translation). In Galatians 2:5, concerning the intruders in the Antioch church, Paul says, "We never yielded to these people for a moment, so that the truth of the gospel (ἡ ἀλήθεια τοῦ εὐαγγελίου) might remain with you (πρὸς ὑμᾶς)" (my translation).[27]

This last phrase, "with you," which addresses the audience of the Epistle to the Galatians, is critical evidence that in Paul's mind what happened to the Antioch church and what is happening to the Galatian church are fundamentally the same in nature. Galatians 2:1–14 provides the Galatian believers with a window through which they can see what happened in the Antioch church and compare it with what is happening in their own church. Through this intentional transparency, Paul successfully demonstrates that the truth of the gospel (ἡ ἀλήθεια τοῦ εὐαγγελίου) that he fought for at the Apostolic Council in Jerusalem and at the Antioch Incident is the same truth that he is trying to defend in this letter to the Galatians.

It is noteworthy that Paul uses the key phrase, *the truth of the gospel* (ἡ ἀλήθεια τοῦ εὐαγγελίου), in Galatians 2:14 in order to characterize the nature of the Antioch Incident. That is to say, in Paul's mind the Antioch Incident is not just about a trivial matter of some eating habit. It is a serious challenge against the universalistic soteriology based on the faith/faithfulness in/of Jesus Christ rather than the works of the Torah, and therefore it is a threat to the truth of the gospel, as Paul understands it. It is in that sense that the confusion caused by the "false brothers," who sneaked into the Antioch church *before* the Apostolic Council in Jerusalem (Gal. 2:4), and the catastrophe caused by "certain people from James," who came to Antioch *after* the Apostolic Council (v. 12), are of the same nature. The Galatian Incident happened in a similar fashion, and thus it has continuity with the Antioch Incident.

This continuity may give us a hint to the identity of the opponents of Paul in Antioch and in Galatia. Even though the "false brothers" (2:4) who sneaked into the Antioch church before the Apostolic Council in Jerusalem, "certain people from James" (v. 12) who came to the Antioch church after the Apostolic Council, and "those who disturbed the Galatian believers" (1:7, my translations) seem to be three different groups of people—and despite the fact that their exact identity remains hidden—we know at least how they are viewed by Paul with regard to their theological stances and their intentions of interfering with his churches. That is, they were Judaizing particularists who believed and taught that the observance of the commandments of the Torah was still necessary for salvation.[28] Their soteriology implies that salvation is only for the Torah-abiding, covenant people of Israel. Gentiles may be saved, but only when they become Jews by going through circumcision and by observing the commandments of the Torah.[29] This kind of soteriology was diametrically opposed to Paul's universalistic soteriology, which was solely based on the grace of God through faith in/of Jesus Christ, not on the "works" of the Torah—and which, therefore, does not discriminate between Jews and Gentiles. That is what he means by the "truth of the gospel."

At this point, it is important to underscore that Paul's expression οὐ δικαιοῦται ἄνθρωπος ἐξ ἔργων νόμου ("a human being is not justified by the works of the law," my translation) in Galatians 2:16 should not be taken as a rejection of the Torah per se. As the neuter plural noun ἔργων in front of νόμου clearly indicates, it is a reference to the observations of the commandments of the Torah, especially the circumcision law, the purity law, the Sabbath laws, and other ceremonial laws.[30] Also, in this phrase Paul seems to be quoting the slogan of his opponents in the Galatian church, who asserted that the Gentile believers were required to do the "works" of the law in order to be saved. In other words, Paul was not denying the validity of the "Jewish soteriology," as if there were such a thing, but he is rejecting one particular form of Jewish soteriology based on a particular understanding of the Torah, which was held by his Judaizing opponents in the churches of Galatia.

The thematic phrase, "the truth of the gospel" (ἡ ἀλήθεια τοῦ εὐαγγελίου), is explicated both in the *propositio* section of the letter (Gal. 2:15–21), which is the *theological* principle of Paul's universalistic soteriology, and in a declarative statement in the *probatio* section (3:26–29), which is the *hermeneutical* implication of the theological principle:[31]

> We ourselves are Jews by birth and not Gentile sinners; yet we know that a person is justified not by the works of the law but through faith in Jesus Christ. And we have come to believe in Christ Jesus, so that we might be justified by faith in Christ, and not by doing the works of the law, because no one will be justified by the works of the law. But if, in our effort to be justified in Christ, we ourselves have been found to be sinners, is Christ then a servant of sin? Certainly not! But if I build up again the very things that I once tore down, then I demonstrate that I am a transgressor. For through the law I died to the law, so that I might live to God. I have been crucified with Christ; and it is no longer I who live, but it is Christ who lives in me. And the life I now live in the flesh I live by faith in the Son of God, who loved me and gave himself for me. I do not nullify the grace of God; for if justification comes through the law, then Christ died for nothing. (Gal. 2:15–21)

> For in Christ Jesus you are all children of God through faith. As many of you as were baptized into Christ have clothed yourselves with Christ. There is no longer Jew or Greek, there is no longer slave or free, there is no longer male and female; for all of you are one in Christ Jesus. And if you belong to Christ, then you are Abraham's offspring, heirs according to the promise. (Gal. 3:26–29)

Thus, by nullifying the ethnic barriers between Jews and Gentiles, Paul presents himself as an innovative Jewish theologian who calls for a radical change in Jewish self-identity. With the coming of Christ there is no longer salvific relevance for the ethnic boundary of the Jews as the covenant people, defined in such terms as the circumcision, the purity law, the Sabbath, and other ceremonial regulations. All humanity is now under the same grace of God through Jesus Christ. With this theological principle of Galatians, we see the emergence of Paul the universalist par excellence.[32]

Because Paul's letter to the Galatians is the only available source of information about the Galatian Incident, there is no way for us to know how effective the letter was when it was delivered and read to the Galatian believers.[33] Paul mentions "Galatia" only once in his other letters: First Corinthians 16:1 says, "Now concerning the collection for the saints: you should follow the directions I gave to the churches of Galatia." Even if 1 Corinthians was written after Galatians, as I believe it was, that statement alone does not tell us anything about the aftermath of the Galatian Incident because the instruction could have been given them either before or after the incident. In contrast, the fact that Paul does not mention the Galatian church as one of the actual contributors to the collection in 2 Corinthians 8 and 9 may indicate that the Galatian Incident resulted in a permanent breach between Paul and the Galatian believers.

On the other hand, Acts 18:23 says, "After spending some time there he departed and went from place to place through the region of Galatia and Phrygia, strengthening all the disciples." This functions as a flashback to the same geographical references in Acts 16:6, which we took as the occasion of Paul's founding the Galatian church. So, if Acts 18:23 is historical, which is difficult to assess, it might be taken as an indication that reconciliation was finally reached between Paul and the Galatian believers. However, even the Lukan text in Acts 18:23 does not actually say that Paul visited the churches of Galatia, and therefore it does not provide any positive evidence for the putative reconciliation. Also, the fact that Galatians was preserved and included in the Pauline corpus may give additional support to the conjecture that the Galatians were indeed persuaded by the letter and were won back to Paul. Nevertheless, the preservation of the letter alone should not be taken as a decisive clue, because there could be many different ways and reasons for an ecclesiastical letter to have survived and to be preserved. What we do know from other letters of Paul is that, no matter what the immediate result of the Galatian Incident was, the interference of Jewish particularists with Pauline churches against his universalistic soteriology did not stop there,[34] as we will see in the next chapter.

Chapter 5

Paul's Ephesian Stay and the Corinthian Incident

PAUL'S EARLY CORRESPONDENCE WITH CORINTH

The next residential ministry of Paul after his Corinthian stay was in Ephesus, the capital of the Roman province of Asia. Acts 18:18–19:1 has a detailed itinerary of Paul after his departure from the Corinthian church: Corinth to Ephesus to Caesarea to (Jerusalem)[1] to Antioch[2] to Galatia and Phrygia to Ephesus. None of these short visits can be confirmed by Paul's own letters except for the fact that he stayed in Ephesus for a period of time after he left Corinth[3] and that he apparently wrote 1 Corinthians from there (cf. 1 Cor. 16:8, 19). The content of 1 Corinthians indicates that Paul maintained close contact with the Corinthian church after his departure from Corinth, which may suggest that Paul's move from Corinth to Ephesus was a fairly recent one.

First Corinthians 5:9 reveals that Paul had written at least once to the Corinthian church before he wrote 1 Corinthians, but the communication between Paul and Corinth prior to 1 Corinthians was not just through letters. We know from 1 Corinthians that, on one occasion, the members of Chloe's household (1:11) and, on another, Stephanas, Fortunatus, and Achaicus as the representatives of the Corinthian church (16:17) brought information to Paul about the current situations of the Corinthian church.

Even though 1 Corinthians mostly deals with internal problems within the church, which are not directly related to the subject matter of this book, there are in this letter a few allusions to some form of opposition to Paul in the Corinthian church (cf. 1 Cor. 4:3, 18–19; 9:1–27; 15:1–11). These verses give us only a partial picture of what was going on in the Corinthian church and the identity of the opponents, if there were any, remains hidden.[4] However, some criticisms against Paul can still be reconstructed from these verses. First of all, 1 Corinthians 9:3 reveals that Paul himself was aware of the criticisms leveled against his apostleship in the Corinthian church, which is why he felt compelled to write his defense statement (ἀπολογία).[5] Paul's rhetorical question in 1 Corinthians 9:1a, "Am I not an apostle?" (οὐκ εἰμὶ ἀπόστολος;), expects an answer in the affirmative,[6] and it probably alludes to an actual charge from his opponents that he was not a legitimate apostle. The following verses (vv. 1b–2) imply that the core of this charge was that Paul was not qualified to be an apostle because he had not seen the Lord and his self-asserted apostleship was never officially sanctioned by the Jerusalem authorities. In defense of his apostleship Paul maintained that he had indeed seen the risen Christ (cf. 9:1b; 15:8) and that he did not need Jerusalem's endorsement because his apostleship was directly from God.[7] Unfortunately, however, both of these defense statements of Paul could easily be (and probably were) dismissed by his opponents. Thus, Paul tended to find himself in a vulnerable position with regard to the question of his apostleship. Nevertheless, he still seems to be confident about his authority as the pastoral leader of the church, as is clear from his instruction on how to raise the collection money, his future plans to visit them, and his exhortations in 1 Corinthians 16.

While we do not know the identity of Paul's opponents in the Corinthian church, we do see his response to them. Their stance led Paul to put forward the theological principle of his mission strategies, a principle rooted in his universalistic soteriology. For example, he writes:

> Was anyone at the time of his call already circumcised? Let him not seek to remove the marks of circumcision. Was anyone at the time of his call uncircumcised? Let him not seek circumcision. Circumcision is nothing, and uncircumcision is nothing; but obeying the commandments of God is everything. Let each of you remain in the condition in which you were called. (1 Cor. 7:18–20) [8]

> For though I am free with respect to all, I have made myself a slave to all, so that I might win more of them. To the Jews I became as a Jew, in order to win Jews. To those under the law I became as one under the law (though I myself am not under the law) so that I might win those under the law. To those outside the law I became as one outside the law (though I am not free from God's law but am under Christ's law) so that I might win those outside the law. To the weak I became weak, so that I might win the weak. I have become all things to all people, that I might by all means save some. I do it all for the sake of the gospel, so that I may share in its blessings. (1 Cor. 9:19–23)

With these verses Paul tells the Corinthian believers that being a Jew has lost its salvific significance.[9] The church of Christ is universal, transcending the ethnic boundaries of Jews and Gentiles.[10] Thus, Paul declares that Jewish particularism is now outdated and there is no place for Judaizers in Pauline churches—or in any church of Christ for that matter.

We cannot be sure of the effect this letter may have had with regard to the specific problems it addresses, because there is no clear information as to how the letter was received by various groups of people in the Corinthian church. It was only afterwards that the relation between Paul and the Corinthian believers became really sour, as 2 Corinthians shows us.

THE OPPONENTS OF PAUL IN 2 CORINTHIANS

As to what happened after 1 Corinthians was written and received, we have no other source of information than 2 Corinthians, which contains only indirect references and allusions to Paul's opposition. Therefore, any attempt to identify the opponents of Paul in the Corinthian church must remain hypothetical.[11] The most important passage in 2 Corinthians with regard to the identity of Paul's opponents is 2 Corinthians 11:22–23:

> Are they Hebrews? So am I. Are they Israelites? So am I. Are they descendants of Abraham? So am I. Are they ministers of Christ? I am talking like a madman—I am a better one.

If these are Paul's counterclaims to the boastings of his opponents, as they seem to be, we may at least infer that the opponents of Paul were self-consciously ethnic Jews who became believers, and then ministers of Christ, and who still regarded the descent from Abraham as a decisive element of their identity. Also, 2 Corinthians 11:4–5 reveals Paul's perception of their theological outlook:

> For if someone comes and proclaims another Jesus than the one we proclaimed, or if you receive a different spirit from the one you received, or a different gospel from the one you accepted, you submit to it readily enough. I think that I am not in the least inferior to these super-apostles.

In Paul's judgment, his opponents in the Corinthian church preached a different Jesus, a different spirit, and a different gospel from the ones he himself preached. Theologically speaking, the phrase, "a different gospel" ($\epsilon\dot{\upsilon}\alpha\gamma\gamma\dot{\epsilon}\lambda\iota\upsilon\nu$ $\ddot{\epsilon}\tau\epsilon\rho\upsilon\nu$) in 2 Corinthians 11:4 is the umbrella term, under which "another Jesus" and "a different spirit" can be put together as part of its content.[12] This reference to "a different gospel" ($\epsilon\dot{\upsilon}\alpha\gamma\gamma\dot{\epsilon}\lambda\iota\upsilon\nu$ $\ddot{\epsilon}\tau\epsilon\rho\upsilon\nu$)[13] unmistakably harks back to the exact same phrase in Galatians 1:6. In fact, the tone and the language of 2 Corinthians 11:4–5 are also remarkably similar to those of Galatians 1:6. Furthermore, in 2 Corinthians 11:5 and 13, Paul calls his opponents "super-apostles" ($\upsilon\dot{\iota}$ $\dot{\upsilon}\pi\epsilon\rho\lambda\dot{\iota}\alpha\nu$ $\dot{\alpha}\pi\dot{\upsilon}\sigma\tau\upsilon\lambda\upsilon\iota$) and "false apostles" ($\psi\epsilon\upsilon\delta\alpha\pi\dot{\upsilon}\sigma\tau\upsilon\lambda\upsilon\iota$), terms that again resonate with a similar expression, "false brothers" ($\psi\epsilon\upsilon\delta\dot{\alpha}\delta\epsilon\lambda\phi\upsilon\iota$) in Galatians 2:4. All these verbal parallels between Galatians and 2 Corinthians make it clear that Paul sees his opponents in the Corinthian church as essentially the same as his opponents in the Galatian churches with regard to their theology and kerygma. They all preach the "other" gospel—that is, the gospel of the circumcision—and it is based on their particularistic soteriology. They are Judaizers who force the observation of the commandments of the Torah on Gentile believers.[14]

THE COURSE OF EVENTS

The course of events in the Corinthian church that underlies 2 Corinthians is very difficult to reconstruct because the information about it comes solely from a few references and allusions in the text of 2 Corinthians itself. What makes the task even more difficult is that 2 Corinthians is a very complex document in terms of its literary composition.

First of all, there are many instances of literary seams or disjunctures that prevent smooth flow of the text. For example, 2 Corinthians 6:14–7:1 is out of context in terms of its connection with both the preceding pericope and the following one. Once this literary anomaly is recognized, it is easy to realize that 2 Corinthians 6:13 connects far better with 7:2 than with 6:14, especially through the use of the "heart" imagery that runs from 6:11 to 6:13 and 7:2.[15]

> In return—I speak as to children—open wide your hearts also (πλατύν-θητε καὶ ὑμεῖς). (6:13)

> Make room in your hearts for us (χωρήσατε ἡμᾶς); we have wronged no one, we have corrupted no one, we have taken advantage of no one. (7:2)

Likewise, 2 Corinthians 2:12–13 connects better with 7:5 than with 2:14, because of the mention of Macedonia:

> When I came to Troas to proclaim the good news of Christ, a door was opened for me in the Lord; but my mind could not rest because I did not find my brother Titus there. So I said farewell to them and went on to Macedonia. (2:12–13)

> For even when we came into Macedonia, our bodies had no rest, but we were afflicted in every way—disputes without and fears within. (7:5)

These and other similar examples make us wonder if some parts of the document were dislocated from their original contexts. Second, the bitter and sarcastic language that dominates 2 Corinthians 10–13 sets this section apart from the rest of the document (chaps. 1–9), in which Paul is either hopeful for the possibility of reconciliation or happy about the reconciliation that has already happened.

In order to account for these literary peculiarities of 2 Corinthians, many different partition theories have been proposed. Even though there is no scholarly consensus as to the number of hypothetical fragments that make up the current canonical text of 2 Corinthians and the way they should be rearranged, the majority of scholars accept the fundamental premise of the partition theory of 2 Corinthians and many of them agree that at least 2 Corinthians 10–13 is a separate letter fragment, although less agreement exists concerning the partition hypothesis for 2 Corinthians 1–9. This is not a place for detailed discussions on this particular issue.[16] So, without going into elaborate arguments, I will adopt the so-called "Six Letter Hypothesis" as a working hypothesis for the literary composition of 2 Corinthians, according to which the fragments are rearranged in their presumable chronological order as follows:[17]

1. A Non-Pauline (?) Interpolation (6:14–7:1)[18]
2. The First Apologia (2:14–6:13; 7:2–4)
3. The Letter of Tears (10:1–13:14)
4. The Letter of Reconciliation (1:1–2:13; 7:5–16)
5. A Letter to the Corinthian Church for the Resumption of the Collection (8:1–24)
6. A Letter to the Churches of Achaia for the Collection (9:1–15)

These six fragments—with the possible exception of 2 Corinthians 6:14–7:1, for which Pauline authorship is disputed—were written by Paul between 1 Corinthians and Romans. The course of events surrounding these fragments is hypothetically reconstructed as follows.

The Initial Attack of the Opponents and Paul's First Apologia (2 Cor. 2:14–6:13; 7:2–4)

Some time after Paul wrote 1 Corinthians, the opponents of Paul in the Corinthian church, most probably Judaizing intruders, launched a systematic attack on Paul's apostleship and his gospel.[19] As was the case with the Galatian Incident, the Judaizing opponents of Paul came to a Pauline church in Paul's absence and tried to overturn what he had done. Also, as in the Galatian Incident, they seem to have been successful in persuading the local believers. Paul heard of this incident while he was still staying in Ephesus. As was his custom, he immediately wrote to the believers a letter of apologia (2 Cor. 2:14–6:13; 7:2–4) in defense of the gospel he preached and his apostleship. This apologia is similar to Galatians in nature and purpose. It is from this letter fragment that we can reconstruct some of the criticisms that Paul's opponents heaped on him, as well as his responses to them.

We notice here that the nature of the attack from Paul's opponents in 2 Corinthians is harsher than that in Galatians. Moreover, the criticisms against Paul in 2 Corinthians are often ad hominem, which was not the case with Galatians. Accordingly, Paul's counterattack is also pretty pungent. In fact, there is an escalating degree of harshness of the attack against Paul by his opponents as the course of events evolves from the Antioch Incident to the Galatian Incident and to the Corinthian Incident. In the Antioch Incident, the intruders did not deny the validity of the gospel of the uncircumcision per se, nor did they challenge Paul's authority. In the Galatian Incident, Paul's opponents denied the salvific efficacy of the gospel of the uncircumcision and discredited Paul's apostleship. In the Corinthian Incident, Paul's opponents denied the gospel of the uncircumcision, rejected Paul's apostleship, and even launched ad hominem attacks on Paul's personality and integrity.

Apart from the usual charge that Paul was not qualified to be an apostle because he had not been an eyewitness of the ministry of Jesus, the opponents seem to have accused Paul and his colleagues of being "peddlers of the word of God" (οἱ καπηλεύοντες τὸν λόγον τοῦ θεοῦ, 2 Cor. 2:17, my translation), which is probably a hostile reference to his effort in Corinth to raise the collection money for the Jerusalem church (1 Cor. 16:1–4).[20] They also seem to have pointed out that Paul did not have a letter of recommendation (ἐπιστολὴ συστατική) from the Jerusalem church (2 Cor. 3:1–3), which might have been viewed as necessary to validate one's apostleship. Certainly the letter of recommendation was a well-established convention in Greco-Roman society as well as in Jewish society.[21] For example, when Roman imperial delegates were sent to provinces, they would normally carry with them a letter of recommendation bearing the imperial seal in order to verify their identity. For the same purpose, the "apostles" (שְׁלִיחִים) of the high priest in Jerusalem would likewise take with them an official letter of recommendation, sealed by the authority of the high priest, when they went around visiting Diaspora synagogues to collect the temple tax. Needless to say, a major function of these letters of recommendation was to prevent fraudulent claims by impersonators of various kinds. The opponents of Paul in 2 Corinthians may very well have shown the Corinthian believers letters of recommendation written on their behalf and sealed by James or other Jerusalem apostles,[22] subsequently arguing that the failure on Paul's part to do the same proved the illegitimacy of his apostleship.

To such a charge Paul could only answer, "Surely we do not need, as some do, letters of recommendation to you or from you, do we? You yourselves are our letter, written on our hearts, to be known and read by all" (2 Cor. 3:1b–2). The juxtaposition of letters written on paper and letters written on the heart is not just an ad hoc tactic on Paul's part; rather, it is a representation of his fundamental hermeneutical dualism of "letter vs. spirit" (2 Cor. 3:6), which is consistently applied to his interpretation of the Torah. In any case, this defensive rhetoric of Paul, wonderful as it may sound, turned out to be completely ineffective in the presence of people who demanded nothing other than hard proof.

The rest of 2 Corinthians 3 shows indirectly what kind of theological arguments the opponents made and how Paul responded to them. In 2 Corinthians 3:6 Paul identifies himself and his fellow workers as ministers of a "new covenant (καινὴ διαθήκη), not of letter but of spirit." The juxtaposition is clearly between the particularistic soteriology of his Judaizing opponents based on the old covenant (παλαιὰ διαθήκη, 2 Cor. 3:14) according to the letter of the Torah and his own universalistic soteriology based on the new covenant (καινὴ διαθήκη) in spirit. Paul then declares, "The letter (τὸ γράμμα) kills, but the Spirit (τὸ πνεῦμα) gives life" (2 Cor. 3:6). The metaphoric expression "kills" (ἀποκτείνει) is certainly a hyperbole. It refers to the old soteriology based on the literal observance of the commandments of the Torah, which Paul believed was no longer salvifically effective. It is in that sense that Paul says, "The letter kills." As far as Paul did not reject the Scripture as such, the Torah itself certainly remained valid, but the "letters" (γράμματα) of the Torah now needed a radically new interpretation. That is, the old covenant should now be understood from the vantage point of what God has done through Jesus Christ (v. 14), which ensures freedom from the bondage of the law (v. 17)[23] and therefore transcends the ethnic barriers between Jews and Gentiles. This cosmic dimension of the new soteriology is further emphasized by 2 Corinthians 5:19 ("In Christ God was reconciling the world to himself, not counting their trespasses against them, and entrusting the message of reconciliation to us"). Therefore, the old literal interpretation of the scripture does not give life; the new "spiritual" interpretation does. This *hermeneutical dualism* of Paul, which parallels his anthropological dualism of flesh (σάρξ) and spirit (πνεῦμα), is part of the foundation of Paul's universalism.[24]

Second Corinthians 5:16 ("From now on, therefore, we regard no one from a human point of view; even though we once knew Christ from a human point of view, we know him no longer in that way") can also be interpreted as Paul's defense against the opponents' charge that he cannot be an apostle because he is not an eyewitness of Jesus. The phrase, "to know Christ according to flesh" is ambiguous. Grammatically speaking, the phrase κατὰ σάρκα can belong either with the verb ἐγνώκαμεν or with the object Χριστόν. The former, γινώσκειν (Χριστὸν) κατὰ σάρκα, would mean "to know (Christ) by direct contact"; the latter, (γινώσκειν) Χριστὸν κατὰ σάρκα, would mean "(to know) the Christ in flesh, i.e., in his earthly existence"—that is, "(to know) the historical Jesus," if I may borrow the language of our time. Either way, it would still require firsthand contact with Jesus, which Paul did not have. By inference, the opposite of γινώσκειν Χριστὸν κατὰ σάρκα would be γινώσκειν Χριστὸν κατὰ πνεῦμα.[25] Even though this sentence is not there on the surface of the text, its idea certainly lies in the background. Thus, Paul here implicitly contrasts between eyewitnessing the earthly Jesus and encountering the risen Christ through revelation, and he privileges the latter, which alone he could claim for himself (1 Cor. 15:8; Gal. 1:16). Thus the *epistemological dualism* that Paul employs here also serves as a foundation for legitimizing his apostleship.

Then in the following section (2 Cor. 5:17–21) Paul restates his soteriology in a more positive tone by emphasizing the newness of God's salvific work through Christ. Second Corinthians 5:17 is the title sentence: "If anyone is in Christ, there is a new creation (καινὴ κτίσις)." According to Galatians 6:15 ("For neither circumcision counts for anything, nor uncircumcision, but a new creation," my translation), the new creation (καινὴ κτίσις) in Christ transcends the boundary between circumcision and uncircumcision. Most probably, that is part of the connotation of 2 Corinthians 5:17.

It is noteworthy that Paul repeatedly used the language of *reconciliation* (καταλλαγή) to articulate the essential premise of his soteriology here (2 Cor. 5:18–20). As Romans 5:10–11 shows, reconciliation is indeed a key concept of Paul's understanding of what salvation is about. However, it is certainly not coincidental that Paul profusely used the expression of reconciliation in 2 Corinthians 5:18–20, because what he desired to achieve through this apologetic letter was reconciliation between the Corinthian believers and himself.[26] As for the prospect of reconciliation, Paul seems to have been quite optimistic, at least up to this point, as is shown by his forthright plea for the Corinthian believers to accept him back (6:11–13; 7:2–4).

Paul would soon realize, however, that he was too naïve. As the other fragments will clearly show, his first letter of apologia did not achieve the desired effect.[27] The Corinthian believers were still not convinced by his defense speech. Disillusioned by the news of the failure of his letter, Paul decided to go there in person and deal with the problem face to face. Hence, his second, "interim" visit to the Corinthian church.

Paul's Interim Visit to Corinth and the Letter of Tears (2 Cor. 10:1–13:14)

Both 2 Corinthians 10:1–13:14 and 1:1–2:13; 7:5–16 have references to Paul's short intermediate visit to the Corinthian church, a trip that is not mentioned in Acts.[28] First of all, 2 Corinthians 13:2 has a specific reference to this "second" visit: ὡς παρὼν τὸ δεύτερον καὶ ἀπὼν νῦν. In 2 Corinthians 2:1, Paul retrospectively talks about his earlier "painful visit" (ἐν λύπῃ . . . ἐλθεῖν) to Corinth. This intermediate visit of Paul must have been a disastrous one. It seems that there was someone in the Corinthian church who openly wronged Paul during his interim visit (ὁ ἀδικήσας, 7:12) and that the wrongdoer and his supporters prevailed (13:2). We do not know exactly what happened there nor who the wrongdoer was.[29] He was either one of Paul's Judaizing opponents, alluded to in 2 Corinthians 11:22–23, or one of the members of the Corinthian church who was persuaded by Paul's opponents. In any case, Paul was so hurt by this event that he was determined, at least at that time, not to visit them again ("I made up my mind not to make you another painful visit," 2:1). Second Corinthians 12:14 shows, however, that Paul later had a change of heart and that he was again ready to visit them "this third time" (τρίτον τοῦτο). This statement would make sense only if there had been a "second" visit of Paul to the Corinthian church, a visit that is often called an "interim" in the sense that it happened between Paul's foundation visit and his last stay in Corinth.[30]

After this sorrowful interim visit to the Corinthian church Paul returned to Ephesus. Then, apparently before he completely recuperated from the trauma of the disastrous visit, he wrote an emotionally charged letter—the so-called "Letter of Tears" to the Corinthian believers (2 Cor. 10–13). Later, in his Letter of Reconciliation (1:1–2:13; 7:5–16), Paul makes a retrospective reference to this emotional letter by saying, "For I wrote you out of much distress and anguish of heart and with many tears (διὰ πολλῶν δακρύων)" (2:4). The purpose of this Letter of Tears was to achieve what Paul's interim visit failed to achieve: it was meant to defend himself and his apostleship against the charges of his opponents and to win back the Corinthian believers to his side. The language of this letter is full of sarcasm (e.g., 10:1; 11:7–8, 16–18; 12:13) and irony (e.g., 11:19–21, 30; 12:10–11),[31] which honestly reflects the state of Paul's mind at the time of writing this letter. Nevertheless, Paul still wrote with careful rhetorical considerations, as the effect of this letter will demonstrate.

The Letter of Tears contains quotations of and allusions to the accusations by Paul's opponents against him, as well as what they claimed for themselves. In 2 Corinthians 10:10 Paul quotes his opponents as saying, "His [Paul's] letters are weighty and strong, but his bodily presence is weak, and his speech contemptible." Similarly, Paul's opponents also seem to have said Paul was untrained in speech (ἰδιώτης τῷ λόγῳ, 11:6), and some of them may even have said Paul was a fool (ἄφρων, v. 16). They probably made a charge that Paul had no spiritual experiences, which he felt the need to counter by "boasting" of the visions and revelations he had experienced, albeit in oblique language (12:1–10). Paul's sarcastic remarks regarding his own practice of not receiving any monetary support from the Corinthian church (11:7–9; 12:13) indicate that even this honorable practice had been perverted into a point of criticism by his opponents. Though the exact rhetoric of the opponents' charge cannot be reconstructed with any degree of certainty, it seems probable that they either appealed to the notion that manual labor is demeaning or to the comparison that other legitimate apostles were financially supported by the church as they were entitled.[32]

As noted before, 2 Corinthians 11:21b–23 indicates that the opponents of Paul boasted of their ethnic identity as Jews, claiming to be Hebrews (Ἑβραῖοι), Israelites (Ἰσραηλῖται), and descendants of Abraham (σπέρμα Ἀβραάμ). They apparently saw this heritage as *soteriologically* important. From this ethnocentric perspective, they preached "another Jesus," "a different spirit," and "a different gospel" from the ones that Paul preached (v. 4). The phrase, "different gospel" (εὐαγγέλιον ἕτερον), is also found in Galatians 1:6, where it most likely refers to the "gospel of the circumcision" (Gal. 2:7), which Paul saw as necessarily leading to the "bondage" of law. Accordingly, the verb "to enslave" (καταδουλοῦν) in 2 Corinthians 11:20 may very well be interpreted as meaning "to enslave into bondage of the law"—especially given that the verb means the same in Galatians 2:4, which is the only other occurrence of this word in the entire corpus of Paul's letters.

The opponents of Paul in 2 Corinthians presumably identified themselves as "ministers of Christ" (διάκονοι Χριστοῦ, 2 Cor. 11:23) and as "apostles of Christ" (ἀπόστολοι Χριστοῦ, v. 13). They may even have claimed to be "super-apostles" (οἱ ὑπερλίαν ἀπόστολοι, 2 Cor. 11:5), whether or not this is exactly the title they used for themselves. Paul, who no longer acknowledged the validity of "the other gospel" (Gal. 1:7), categorically judged them as "false apostles" (ψευδαπόστολοι, 2 Cor. 11:13). He even intimated that they were "Satan's ministers" (v. 15). Such harsh language of Paul in this letter again resembles that of Galatians 1:8–9.

All these parallels between Galatians and 2 Corinthians lead to the conclusion that there is a fundamental theological continuity between Paul's opponents in

Galatia and those in Corinth, at least in his perception of them. In both cases, it is a battle between Paul and his opponents who are using the same kinds of weapons. Moreover, as we consistently see, this conflict represents the paradigmatic tension between particularism and universalism within early Christianity during the period prior to the separation of Christianity from Judaism.

Paul in Macedonia and the Letter of Reconciliation (2 Cor. 1:1–2:13; 7:5–16)

Second Corinthians 12:20–21 reveals Paul's anxieties about how his letter will be received by the Corinthian believers. Having experienced the failure of his First Letter of Apologia and another painful failure of his second visit to the Corinthian church, he was no longer confident about the prospect of winning the Corinthian believers back to his side. So, with an implicit threat to exercise his authority to tear them down (καθαίρεσις, 13:10) as a last resort in the hypothetically worst-case scenario, Paul finally pleads with them to listen to his appeal (παρακαλεῖσθε, 13:11),[33] which I take as a metatextual reference to the entire Letter of Tears. As the later references in the Letter of Reconciliation suggest (2:13; 7:6, 13–14), the Letter of Tears was entrusted to Titus for delivery, who had previously been sent to Corinth for a task (12:18). Titus's commission would probably have included reporting back to Paul concerning the reception of the letter and the reaction of the Corinthian believers to it. It appears that Titus was scheduled to come back to report to Paul in Ephesus from Corinth via Macedonia and Troas, which would be a natural inland route.

In 2 Corinthians 2:12–13, which seems to refer to a time not long after Paul sent Titus to Corinth with the Letter of Tears, Paul talks about his trip to Troas and his subsequent move to Macedonia. According to what he says in verse 13, the purpose of this trip was to find Titus. Apparently, being too anxious to hear from Titus, Paul could no longer stay back in Ephesus. So he left Ephesus[34] and went to Troas presumably in an attempt to get closer to Corinth, from which Titus was supposed to travel. Paul might even have felt the urge to go all the way to Corinth to find out what the result was, but after two consecutive failures he could no longer dare to go there in person. So he stopped midway, at Troas.

Concerning how he was feeling at that time, Paul says, "When I came to Troas to proclaim the good news of Christ, a door was opened for me in the Lord; but my mind could not rest because I did not find my brother Titus there" (2 Cor. 2:12–13a). So Paul traveled on to Macedonia, which was still closer to Corinth, in order to wait for Titus to come (2:13b). This travel of Paul from Ephesus to Macedonia is briefly mentioned in Acts 20:1, albeit without any hint of the underlying circumstances ("After the uproar ceased, Paul sent for the disciples and having exhorted them took leave of them and departed for Macedonia," my translation). Again, in 2 Corinthians 7:5, which originally connected with 2:13 according to the partition theory we adopted, Paul recalls how he felt at that time: "For even when we came into Macedonia, our bodies had no rest, but we were afflicted in every way—disputes without and fears within." Obviously, Paul could no longer be naïvely optimistic about the result of his Letter of Tears. So, neither his mind nor his body found rest. He was, so to speak, psychosomatically ill.

Finally, a great relief came to Paul. Titus came at last and brought him the good news that the Letter of Tears achieved its desired effect: the reconciliation between Paul and the Corinthian believers. In 2 Corinthians 7:6–7, Paul recalls this joyous moment of hearing from Titus about the dramatic turn of events in the Corinthian church:

> But God, who consoles the downcast, consoled us by the arrival of Titus, and not only by his coming, but also by the consolation with which he was consoled about you, as he told us of your longing, your mourning, your zeal for me, so that I rejoiced still more.

The Corinthian believers, who had once rejected Paul and humiliated him in many ways, now repented, felt sorry about what they had done to him, and were longing to see him again. Obviously, the rhetoric of the Letter of Tears worked. It achieved what Paul's personal presence could not. After all, his opponents were not entirely wrong when they said, "His letters are weighty and strong, but his bodily presence is weak" (2 Cor. 10:10).

In the joy of having been reconciled with the Corinthian believers, Paul immediately wrote the Letter of Reconciliation from Macedonia—a letter that is partially preserved in 2 Corinthians 1:1–2:13 and 7:5–16, according to the partition theory adopted in this book. In this warmhearted letter, Paul repeatedly mentions the words "to console" (παρακαλεῖν) and "consolation (παράκλησις) from affliction (θλῖψις)," which must have dominated his feelings at that time.[35] He says those afflictions were for their salvation (σωτηρία, 2 Cor. 1:6), which means that in his view nothing less than the salvation of the Corinthian believers was at stake during the whole course of events. This had been a battle between two different gospels with two different soteriologies, of which Paul believed, at least at that moment, only one could be true.

In retrospect, Paul also mentions here his second, "painful" visit (2 Cor. 2:1–4), in which he was wronged by one of them, and he urges the Corinthian believers to forgive that opponent his wrong, since Paul himself has already forgiven him (2 Cor. 2:5–11). Paul is even a little apologetic about the harsh tone of his previous Letter of Tears, although he is glad that he wrote as he did, because its rhetoric eventually produced the desired result (7:8–13a). Now Paul rejoices because he is completely confident in the Corinthian believers (v. 16). In the end, his universalistic soteriology won a decisive victory in Corinth over against the particularist soteriology of his opponents.

Chapter 6

Paul's Effort
for the Unity of the Church

RESUMPTION OF THE COLLECTION PROJECT

The reconciliation with the Corinthian church must have been a great relief for Paul and it seems to have offered him a time of reflection, in which he could critically assess his apostolic work in the past few years and draw a prospect for his future ministry. The series of incidents at Antioch, Galatia, and Corinth had forced Paul to be on the defensive with regard to his apostleship and the gospel he preached. Having to be defensive on theological matters often causes one to become more rigid and less flexible in thinking than he or she would otherwise be. That is probably what was happening to Paul, when he declared to the Galatian believers that there could be no other gospel than the one he preached (Gal. 1:7) and when he slurred his Jewish Christian opponents in the Corinthian church as "false apostles" and even "ministers of Satan [implied]" (2 Cor. 11:13–15).

This austere position of Paul virtually revoked the agreement of the Apostolic Council in Jerusalem, which had sanctioned the two gospels (i.e., the gospel of the circumcision and the gospel of the uncircumcision) as equally valid. Paul himself was happy about that agreement. Facing an extreme situation in the Galatian church, however, he reversed himself and denied the validity of any gospel other than his. Even though it is true that Paul was only fighting back against his opponents who had first breached the ethos of the Jerusalem agreement, that does not make him any less culpable for the kind of exclusive attitude he showed in Galatians 1:6–7 and 2 Corinthians 11:4, 13–15. Moreover, this kind of exclusive attitude conflicts with the strategic as well as theological principle of flexibility that he himself articulates in 1 Corinthians 9:19–23. It also undermines his own theological principle that love is more important than dogmatic correctness (1 Cor. 8:1–3). I will argue later that this exclusive stance of Paul was an unfortunate outcome of his struggle with his Judaizing opponents and that it did not last for the rest of his life.

The most tragic consequence of all these incidents in Antioch, Galatia, and Corinth was that the unity of the church was seriously damaged, unity not so much within Pauline churches as between the Jewish Christian church and the Gentile Christian church. Theological differences caused conflicts, and the latter reinforced the former. The spirit of mutual recognition of the Apostolic Council in Jerusalem was shattered in the course of the conflicts between two different gospels—i.e., two different ways of understanding soteriology. Theological diversity was at first honored in principle, but the spirit of mutual respect was not sustained in the real life of the early Christian communities. In such circumstances, the reconciliation between Paul and the Corinthian church, which was only a local episode, could not be regarded as an end to the conflict because a similar incident could happen elsewhere unless a more fundamental solution were made. Paul was no doubt fully aware of this ongoing threat.

While he was savoring the moment of reconciliation with the Corinthian church and at the same time grieving over the broken unity of the larger church, he made an important decision to launch a project that would consume all his time and energy for the rest of his life: the resumption of the collection for the Jerusalem church. Even though he did not specifically mention the issue of broken unity, it is clear that his desire to reconcile with the Jewish Christian church in Judea was the greatest impetus for his decision to resume the collection project as a token of the restored unity between the Jewish Christian church and the Gentile church. According to Galatians 2:10, the collection for the poor in Jerusalem was originally suggested at the Apostolic Council in Jerusalem, and it was the only injunction imposed on Pauline churches[1] to which Paul agreed enthusiastically. In other words, the collection was from the beginning a token of the unity of the church. It must have gradually lost its meaning as the relationship between the Jewish Christian church in Judea and the Gentile Christian church deteriorated and, as a result, it was virtually aborted. Now Paul wanted to resuscitate it.

The fact that Paul chose to resume the collection project after being repeatedly rejected by his Judaizing opponents means that he was determined to take the initiative in reconciling the two conflicting branches of the church. Considering that the conflict was ultimately a theological one, such an attempt by Paul would not be meaningful or effective unless it was accompanied with a willingness on his part to accommodate to the theological position of the other party. In other words, unless Paul was prepared to forgo the exclusive theological stance that he had recently developed (Gal. 1:6–7; 2 Cor. 11:4–5, etc.), and unless the other party would be willing to do the same, there would be no meaning in the token of unity at all. Paul, not being a fool, must have known that. So, even though there is no explicit statement by Paul that he abandoned his exclusive position, it is reasonable to assume that he was willing to do so when he made the decision to take up the collection project again. I will show later that such a changed attitude of Paul is indeed reflected in the language of Romans and Philippians.

Thus, while Paul was still staying in Macedonia, he urged the churches of Thessalonica and Philippi to raise money for Jerusalem again. Paul's statement in 2 Corinthians 8:1–6 implies that the collection project was already well underway in the churches of Macedonia by the time he wrote 2 Corinthians 8–9. We do not know when it first started there, but we learn from Paul that they made contributions far beyond their means (2 Cor. 8:1–4). We also know that the churches of Galatia and Corinth had previously received Paul's instructions on the collection project (1 Cor. 16:1–4). Whether the Galatian churches participated in this resumed collection project after the Galatian Incident is unknown.[2] The lack of positive evidence for their participation may imply that they did not, but we cannot be sure about this.

As for the Corinthian church, the initial fund-raising effort of Paul for Jerusalem was apparently made a scandal by his opponents and, as a result, it was interrupted. Having been reconciled with the Corinthian church, Paul was now eager to resume the collection there as well. According to the partition theory we adopted in this book, 2 Corinthians 8–9 contains two separate letters that Paul wrote for this purpose.[3] Thus, the common subject of 2 Corinthians 8–9 is "concerning the ministry for the saints" (περὶ τῆς διακονίας τῆς εἰς τοὺς ἁγίους) in Jerusalem (8:4; 9:1). Second Corinthians 8 was addressed to the Corinthian church, and 2 Corinthians 9 to other churches in Achaia. The fact that 2 Corinthians 8 urges the Corinthian believers to resume the collection, whereas 2 Corinthians 9 presupposes a substantial progress of it in Achaia leads us to assume that the former was written shortly after the Letter of Reconciliation and the latter some time after the former.[4] Second Corinthians 8:10 implies that the collection project had been launched at the Corinthian church the previous year (ἀπὸ πέρυσι) but was subsequently interrupted by the opposition to Paul. The interval must have been at least several months if we take into account enough time for Paul's first Letter of Apologia, his painful interim visit, his Letter of Tears, his travel to Macedonia, and his Letter of Reconciliation.[5]

Titus and two other delegates of the church were sent by Paul to deliver 2 Corinthians 8 to the Corinthian church (2 Cor. 8:16–19, 22). Titus is not mentioned in 2 Corinthians 9, in which Paul uses only a generic expression, "the brothers" (τοὺς ἀδελφούς), as a reference to the letter carriers (2 Cor. 9:3, 5). The identity of these people remains unknown, although it is likely that the two letters (2 Cor. 8 and 9) were delivered by the same group of people.[6] Since it was a resumption of what had previously been undertaken, we may safely assume that Paul was still holding on to his original intention: that when the collection was completed, he would send appropriate delegates of the participating churches to Jerusalem, while he on his part would move on westward to complete his ultimate mission in Spain, the west end of the then-known world—although he left open the possibility to take the gift to Jerusalem himself, if necessary (1 Cor. 16:1–4). Paul's later statement in Romans 15:26 shows that these two letters to the Corinthian church and to other churches in Achaia, which pleaded for the collection, were indeed successful and a significant amount of money was ready to be sent to Jerusalem.

PAUL'S LAST VISIT TO CORINTH

As he had said he would in his letter (2 Cor. 12:14; cf. 13:1), Paul finally went from Macedonia to Greece to visit the Corinthian church for the third time (cf. Acts 20:2–3). This visit would turn out to be his last. According to 1 Corinthians 16:5–7, Paul had wished to visit the Corinthian church via Macedonia in order to collect the money raised for the Jerusalem church and to be sent by the Corinthian church to wherever he was heading.[7] This original plan of Paul's was obviously not intended to be carried out at his second, "painful" visit to Corinth, but it was now to be fulfilled at his third visit.

Acts 20:2–3 has only a passing remark about Paul's travel to Greece (εἰς τὴν Ἑλλάδα) and his three-month stay there. No explicit reference to this third and last visit of Paul to Corinth is found in his letters, but Romans, which was most probably written in Corinth, contains a passage that states what he had in mind when he wrote this letter (Rom. 15:14–33). This passage reveals what Paul ultimately wished to achieve for the rest of his career as a "minister of Christ Jesus to the Gentiles" (λειτουργὸς Χριστοῦ Ἰησοῦ εἰς τὰ ἔθνη, Rom. 15:16). Paul basically saw his mission as starting from Jerusalem and moving westward (Rom. 15:19). Having come about halfway, Paul now wished to go to Spain via Rome. Then he would have finished his universal mission, because Spain represented the "end of the earth," as it was known to the people in the Mediterranean world at that time.[8]

However, Paul had an even more pressing mission at this point, which was the restoration of the unity of the church by taking the collection money to Jerusalem as a token of reconciliation. Obviously, Paul had by now decided to take the collection to Jerusalem himself instead of entrusting it to other delegates of the contributing churches. So he postponed his desired trip to Rome and Spain and prepared to go to Jerusalem, hoping he would successfully complete this mission of reconciliation in Judea and resume his westward mission to Spain afterwards (Rom. 15:28–29).

At the same time, however, Paul was not naïvely optimistic. He was fully aware of the dangers and risks that he was taking by embarking on this trip to Jerusalem. He wished for reconciliation but he could not make the assumption that the other party wished for the same. He was still regarded as a controversial figure in the "mainstream" Jewish Christian church in Judea and, if he should ever be accused of being a lawbreaker, anything could happen to him. So he was worried and rightly so. That is why he asked the Roman believers, who did not even know him, for an intercessory prayer on his behalf so that his collection gift might be acceptable to the "saints" in Jerusalem (Rom. 15:30–32). The flip side of this prayer request is that Paul saw a living possibility that the Jerusalem Jewish Christians might reject his gesture for peace.[9] If that were to be the case, he knew he was risking not only the chance to complete his mission "to the end of the world" but also his own life.

The fact that Paul's letter to the Romans has a long theological discussion on his gospel of salvation by grace of God through faith/faithfulness (πίστις) in/of Jesus Christ means that soliciting goodwill from the Roman believers for his future mission (Rom. 15:24) was not the only intention of Paul's writing this letter. Considering the fact that among the seven undisputed letters of Paul, Romans is the only one addressed to a church he did not know directly, it is conceivable that the content of the letter was influenced no less by Paul's own circumstances at the time of writing than by the situations of the addressees. If that is the case, the prospect of Paul's impending confrontation with the Christian Jews (as well as non-Christian Jews) in Jerusalem must have been a crucial factor of the *Sitz-im-Leben* of the letter.[10]

Since Paul wanted to restore the spirit of mutual recognition of the Apostolic Council in Jerusalem, it is natural that he expected to have serious theological conversations with the Jewish Christians in Jerusalem concerning the very issue that had caused conflicts in his churches: that is, the tension between the particularistic soteriology of Paul's Judaizing opponents and his own universalistic soteriology. That is why Paul presents his universalistic gospel so unapologetically in Romans 1–8 but at the same time so strongly affirms the salvation of *all* Israel in chapters 9–11 (see esp. Rom. 11:26). The implied audience of this letter could be very large, even including non-Christian Jews.

It is also noteworthy that Paul is much more lenient in his theological stance in Romans than he was in Galatians,[11] in which he categorically denied the validity of the "other gospel" and called his Jewish Christian opponents "false brothers" (ψευδαδέλφους, Gal. 2:4). In other words, Paul was stepping back from his previous, exclusive mentality in Galatians to go even further back in time to the original stance of mutual recognition of the Apostolic Council in Jerusalem. He was preparing himself for another conference in Jerusalem.

PAUL'S JOURNEY TO JERUSALEM
AND THE DELIVERY OF THE COLLECTION

Thus Paul left Corinth for Jerusalem. The long narrative of his journey from Greece to Jerusalem in Acts 20:3–21:15 has no counterpart in Pauline letters. The stories in this Lukan account of Paul's journey have varying degrees of historical reliability,[12] which does not particularly concern us in this book. We are more interested in how Paul was received by the Jerusalem church and how the desired unity of the church was or was not restored by the delivery of the collection. Unfortunately, however, there is not enough historically reliable data to reconstruct what exactly happened when Paul went to Jerusalem. First of all, we have no statement by Paul about the actual delivery of the collection money in Jerusalem. Second, as was pointed out earlier, Acts does not even mention the collection that Paul took to Jerusalem.[13] Therefore, we have no direct help for the course of events. The accounts of the events that led to Paul's arrest and trials at the Roman governor's court in Acts 21:15–26:32 are heavily redactional and do not easily render accurate information. Luke's tendency in Acts to gloss over thorny conflicts in early Christianity by making the parties concerned always conciliatory to each other may have skewed the picture of reality he purports to present in his narratives.

Acts only establishes the fact that Paul's journey to Jerusalem, whatever his purpose was, resulted in his arrest and ultimately his imprisonment in Rome. This warrants the assumption that Paul's mission of reconciliation in Jerusalem did not achieve its intended goal. Also, even though Paul does not say exactly what happened to him in Jerusalem, we have at least one document reflecting the circumstances resulting from his last trip to Jerusalem. If Paul wrote Philippians during his Roman imprisonment, as I believe he did, then he ended up being a prisoner in Rome as a result of his visit to Jerusalem with the collection money. In other words, it was his *fear* rather than his *wish* in Romans 15:30–32 that was fulfilled in his trip to Jerusalem.

The unity of the church was not achieved. The Jerusalem church remained faithful to the gospel of the circumcision and was not willing to endorse the gospel of the uncircumcision that Paul represented.[14] It is clear that by that time the Jerusalem church had virtually regarded the original decision of the Apostolic Council in Jerusalem as invalid. That is the theological reason that they could not receive the collection from Paul, even though it was something they themselves had initially suggested to Paul and Barnabas at the Apostolic Council in Jerusalem (Gal. 2:10).

According to Acts 21:20, there were numerous Jews who believed in Jesus and who were still zealous for the Torah, and they were highly suspicious about Paul. The following stories give us the impression that these "believing Jews" who were zealous for the law, along with nonbelieving Jews (even though they are not specifically mentioned as such in Acts), were responsible for the arrest and trial of Paul. Considering the fact that the Jewish Christian church in Jerusalem held the same view of the salvific efficacy of the observation of the commandments of the Torah as the majority of the other Jews, it is plausible that the "believing" Jews and the nonbelieving Jews in Jerusalem formed a united front against Paul, who they thought was a great apostate advocating the abrogation of the Torah.

Acts 21:20–25 presents James as if he was conciliatory to Paul and was only trying to help him escape from the potential attack of the Jewish Christians who were zealous for the law. The reliability of this account is in question. Reconstructing any picture of the historical James is extremely difficult because there is no direct evidence available for us.[15] Especially, the assessment of the historicity of this particular passage should take into account the overarching tendency of Luke to camouflage embarrassing conflicts in early Christianity and to present an ideal picture of the church in harmony. Even if we were to take the account in Acts 21:20–25 at face value, it would still be clear that James did not willingly take the initiative to embrace Paul's attempt at the unity of the church of Christ by exercising his authority as the leader of the Jerusalem church, which he could have done if he had so wished. As the leader of the law-abiding Jerusalem church, James probably considered affirmation of the continuing validity of the observation of the commandments of the Torah more important than accepting a token of solidarity with the Gentile churches, which he believed did not honor the Torah.

Thus, the desired unity between the Jewish Christian church in Jerusalem and the Gentile churches of Paul was not achieved. From this point on, the gap between the two branches of early Christianity kept growing bigger, until Pauline Christianity eventually gained the upper hand and developed into the "ecumenical" church. The Torah-abiding Jewish Christianity was pushed to the margin and eventually disappeared from history by the fourth century C.E. Had an open-minded theological conversation taken place between Paul and the leaders of the Jerusalem church at his last visit to Jerusalem over the issue of two different gospels in view of the unity of the church, the theology of the "ecumenical" Christian church in the second century C.E. would have been more inclusive of the Jewish aspects of the Christian gospel, as Paul's enthusiastic argument for the salvation for *all* Israel in Romans 9–11 indicates.[16] Also, the ensuing history of the relations between Jews and Christians would have taken a completely different path than it actually did.

PAUL IN ROMAN PRISON

Paul was now in Roman prison. Acts 28:16, 30–31 gives the impression that Paul was under house arrest, but that is difficult to verify. With the assumption that Philippians was written during this last period of Paul's life, we can at least see what Paul had in mind as he faced an impending execution, which he could have avoided if he had not gone to Jerusalem to deliver the collection money. Philippians was occasioned by a visit of Epaphroditus as a "messenger" (ἀπόστολος) of the Philippian church (Phil. 2:25) to Paul.[17] Apparently, he brought Paul some financial support from the church (4:18). This touched Paul deeply, not because of the money, as he says in verses 11 and 17, but because of the love the Philippians showed him. In appreciation of this and previous financial support (vv. 15–17), Paul sent a letter to the Philippians through Epaphroditus (2:28–30). At this moment Paul was not sure whether he would be delivered from the imprisonment or executed (1:19–26). Even though he says it would not matter either way, he did have a strong wish for deliverance (see esp. vv. 19, 25–26).

What is more important for us is how he saw the whole course of events *theologically*, after his effort for reconciliation turned out to be futile. Philippians 1:15–18 presents an image of Paul that is quite different from that of Galatians or the Letter of Tears (2 Cor. 10–13). Even though it is a passage that expresses Paul's personal feeling, it nevertheless represents a significant theological stance that he developed over the course of his resumption of the collection project, his last trip to Jerusalem, his arrest, and his subsequent imprisonment in Rome.[18]

In Philippians 1:15 Paul says, "Some (Τινὲς μέν) proclaim Christ from envy and rivalry, but others (τινὲς δέ) from goodwill." Here, both "some" and "others" refer to Christian preachers, because they all proclaim Christ. Paul continues, "These (οἱ μέν) proclaim Christ out of love, knowing that I have been put here for the defense of the gospel; the others (οἱ δέ) proclaim Christ out of selfish ambition, not sincerely but intending to increase my suffering in my imprisonment" (vv. 16–17). Having traced the course of his struggle in Antioch, Galatia, and Corinth, we can easily see to whom Paul is referring by "these" (οἱ μέν, v. 16) and by "the others" (οἱ δέ, v. 17). The former were the sympathizers of his universalistic gospel; the latter were his Judaizing opponents with whom he contended in Antioch, Galatia, and Corinth. In the past he used to call the latter "false brothers," "false apostles," or even "ministers of Satan," saying that there is no other gospel than what he preached. Now he had come to think differently. He says in Philippians 1:18, "What does it matter? Just this, that Christ is proclaimed in every way, whether out of false motives or true; and in that I rejoice." Paul was no longer interested in staking an exclusive claim for dogmatic correctness. He realized that what truly matters is the greater scope of mission through which Christ is proclaimed. Thus, any of the people to whom Paul and others preached could become Christian as "either Jew or Gentile," and Paul would rejoice in these new brothers and sisters in Christ (cf. Gal. 3:28).

This passage (Phil. 1:18) is in that sense closest to the ethos of Romans (especially chaps. 9–11), which is the latest letter of Paul prior to his Roman imprisonment. Romans 9–11 and Philippians 1:15–18 are probably the passages that reveal Paul at his most theologically mature state. They show that, toward the end of Paul's life, his theology was not only universal in its soteriological orientation but it also had become *inclusive* in scope. During the course of his struggle with his Judaizing opponents he was self-consciously fighting for his universalistic soteriology in order to *include* the Gentiles into God's fold without making them become Jews by receiving circumcision and by observing Jewish laws. The cause was noble, but, in doing so, he became *exclusive* in terms of his attitude toward "the other gospel." The result was no less than the shattered unity of the church. Once Paul realized it, what mattered to him was not who initiated the division but how to restore the unity. It is in that context that he made the decision to make a sacrificial effort for unity by bringing the collection to the Jerusalem church as an offering for reconciliation.

Unfortunately, his offering was not accepted and he ended up in prison as a rejected person. If he ended his life there, his ultimate wish to go to Spain and finish his mission would have to remain unfulfilled. Most of all, reconciliation did not happen and the church was still divided. So, Paul had every reason to be bitter—but he was not, as we can tell from the contents of his last letter, Philippians, which is full of the language of joy (1:4, 25; 2:2; 4:1, etc.) and rejoicing (1:18; 2:17, 18, 28; 3:1; 4:4, 10, etc.). Philippians 1:15–18 makes it especially clear that Paul had already forgiven his Judaizing opponents, who constantly interfered with his churches. He could not have done that without giving up the exclusive theological stance expressed in Galatians 1:6–7. His theological horizon had broadened, and we can trace that movement from Galatians via Romans to Philippians.[19] The theological change in Paul's mind is only implicitly reflected in Romans and Philippians. How he could embrace the validity of the other gospel (i.e., the gospel of the circumcision) and hold it in harmony with his own gospel (i.e., the gospel of the uncircumcision) is not articulated in overtly theological language. Perhaps it was impossible to harmonize the two seemingly contradictory gospels. Even if it were possible, Paul certainly did not have the time to do that before he was executed in Rome. Nevertheless, his language of affirmation for his opponents (Phil. 1:15–18) is more important for the ethos of inclusivity than any elaborate theological argument would be. In that sense, Paul's last effort for the unity of the church through the collection for Jerusalem was not a failure at all. He certainly did not live to see the fruit of his effort in his lifetime in the concrete sense of the word. However, by leaving the inclusive ethos of Philippians 1:15–18 as part of his legacy, he indeed laid the foundation for a truly ecumenical theology in a broad sense of the term. The struggle for inclusivity that Paul went through in various stages of his life—culminating in his final acceptance of two gospels that together welcomed new believers as *either Jew or Gentile*—was not at all in vain.

Chapter 7

The Aftermath

DISINTEGRATION OF THE JERUSALEM CHURCH

With a few passing remarks on the Jerusalem church in Acts 21 the New Testament leaves the rest of the history of this once-leading Christian church untold, and there is not much information about it elsewhere, either. One of the critical events that happened to the Jerusalem church after Paul's last visit was the death of James. According to Josephus (*Ant.* 20.9.1), during the interregnum of the Roman procurators Festus and Albinus (62 C.E.), the high priest Ananus, who was newly appointed by King Agrippa, assembled the Sanhedrin of judges and had James and some others stoned to death on the charge of transgressing the law (παρανομησάντων, *Ant.* 20.9.1). It is not clear what specific law(s) James was accused of having broken, and it would be futile to make conjectures about it here.[1]

What is more important for us is that Josephus reports a subsequent protest by "those who were considered the most fair-minded (ἐπιεικέστατοι) and strict concerning the law (περὶ τοὺς νόμους ἀκριβεῖς)" against this rash act of the high priest, which resulted in his removal from the office (*Ant.* 20.9.1). Josephus was probably referring to the Pharisees here, since "being strict concerning the law" is a typical epithet of that group.[2] The reference that Ananus followed the Sadducean party makes the idea of the Pharisaic protest more plausible. What we can infer from this is that the Torah-abiding Jewish Christian church in Jerusalem under the leadership of James had maintained a rather congenial relation with the Pharisees but not with the Sadducees, and that was beginning to take its toll.

Eusebius also has an extended account of the death of James (*Hist. Eccl.* 2.23.1–25), which includes quotations of Hegesippus (2.23.4–18) and of Josephus (2.23.21–24).[3] It is interesting to notice that in this account of Eusebius

74

"the Jews" ('Ιουδαῖοι) were responsible both for the death of Paul and for that of James (*Hist. Eccl.* 2.23.1), as if all the Jews were indiscriminately against "Christian" leaders.[4] In other words, what was a matter of intramural controversy within the parameter of Judaism in Josephus's account of the death of James became a Jewish oppression against Christianity in Eusebius's version of the same. This is certainly an anachronism on the part of Eusebius, and as such it reflects more of the circumstances of the fourth century C.E. than the historical reality of the first century C.E.. Unfortunately, this kind of anachronistic viewpoint continued to plague the Christian understanding of the relation between Judaism and Christianity.

This polemical viewpoint of Eusebius against the Jews is intensified in his account of the Jewish war (*Hist. Eccl.* 3.5.1–7). Here the destruction of Jerusalem by the Romans is regarded as God's punishment of the Jews for their crimes against Christ and his apostles (*Hist. Eccl.* 3.5.3), and the flight of the Jerusalem church to Pella is interpreted as God's deliverance of the "holy men" (ἁγίων ἀνδρῶν) from disaster. Eusebius is not clear about whether the Jerusalem believers who had fled to Pella returned to Jerusalem after the war. Instead, he later lists the names of all the fifteen bishops of Jerusalem, beginning with James down to the time of the siege of the Jews by Hadrian (*Hist. Eccl.* 4.5.3). The most plausible implication of this list is that those who had fled to Pella did return to Jerusalem and the church there continued to exist. In fact, Epiphanius, a slightly later contemporary of Eusebius, explicitly says that they did (*De Mensuris,* 15). The historicity of the flight of the Jerusalem church to Pella is in question, which is not an immediate concern of this book.[5] However, even if Eusebius and Epiphanius are both correct in this regard, what remains clear is that the Jerusalem church did not last very long. In fact, the silence of Eusebius concerning what happened to them afterwards implies that they eventually disappeared from history, at least by the middle of the second century C.E. After the failure of the Bar Kochba revolt, Hadrian expelled all the Jews from Jerusalem. This would have been a major factor for the demise of the Jerusalem church. It is also clear that even before this formal expulsion of the Jews from Jerusalem, the Jewish Christian church in Jerusalem already lost its prestigious position as the "mother" church, which it had previously enjoyed during the time of James. The so-called mother church of early Christianity was only short-lived, and its end was far from glorious.

As for the theological stance of the post-Jamesian Jerusalem church, it is important to notice that, in his section on the episcopal succession of the fifteen bishops in the Jerusalem church (*Hist. Eccl.* 4.5.3), Eusebius characterizes them as "the bishops from circumcision" (οἱ ἐπίσκοποι ἐκ περιτομῆς). This phrase immediately resonates with a similar phrase, "those from the circumcision party" (οἱ ἐκ περιτομῆς) in Galatians 2:12, which Paul uses to refer to those who were sent to Antioch by James in Jerusalem. This is a strong indication that the Jerusalem church after the Jewish War, if it continued to exist, maintained the Jamesian legacy of particularism with regard to soteriology until it disappeared from history in the second century C.E.

CONTINUED RIVALRY

The disintegration of the Jerusalem church does not mean that the conflict between particularism and universalism in early Christianity was over. Even though the Jerusalem church and its uncontested authority no longer existed, the Jamesian legacy of Torah-abiding Jewish Christianity with particularistic soteriology persisted at least for a while. As the Pauline branch of early Christianity with universalistic soteriology gradually became dominant and formed the nucleus of the emerging "catholic" church, Jewish Christianity was pushed to the periphery. After the separation of Judaism and Christianity, Jewish Christians with a Jamesian bent were marginalized even more, both by the formative rabbinic Judaism and by the "catholic" Christian church. Marginalization made them more defensive and even polemical against their winning competitor, Pauline Christianity.

The antagonism of this post-Jamesian Jewish Christianity against Paul is abundantly attested in their literature. For example, the *Pseudo-Clementines* are a literary corpus produced by Jewish Christians probably in the fourth century C.E. Its two components, *Pseudo-Clementine Homilies* and *Pseudo-Clementine Recognitions*, are generally believed to have derived from an earlier common source.[6] Both these documents are replete with anti-Paulinism.[7] For example, *Pseudo-Clementine Recognitions* has a very interesting section (1.66–70) in which the anti-Paulinism of Jewish Christianity reaches the climax in its absurdity. According to this text, James, as the bishop (*episcopus*) representing the entire church (*cum omni ecclesia*), went up to the temple of Jerusalem to dispute with the leaders of the people concerning Jesus. When he delivered a christological speech, a "certain hostile person" (*homo quidam inimicus*, 1.70.1) appeared and made disturbances to interfere with James's speech. Then he and his people began to massacre believers with the brand from the altar. In the midst of the turmoil, this hostile man (*ille inimicus homo*, 1.70.8) grabbed James and threw him down from the highest point of the stairs of the temple. James was then believed to be dead, which is why the enemy did not attack him again. Later, this attempted murderer of James is unmistakably identified as Paul (1.71.3–4)!

It is difficult to know the place of origin of these documents. Nevertheless, it is made clear that at least some descendants from the Jamesian branch of Jewish Christianity continued to exist after James and Paul died. Because they were marginalized by the then-dominant Gentile Christianity, they became very defensive and produced various kinds of anti-Pauline polemical documents. These reflect not so much the time of James and Paul as the post-Pauline and post-Jamesian period in which they were written.

As Jewish Christianity gradually vanished, Pauline Christianity with its universalistic outlook became the dominant majority of the emerging "catholic" church, with the result that only one of the two gospels in earliest Christianity survived. This waxing of Pauline Christianity and waning of Jewish Christianity largely coincides with the separation of Judaism and Christianity. The ultimate outcome was that what had been an *intra*mural conflict within early Christianity, while it was still within Judaism, turned into an *inter*religious conflict between Judaism and later Christianity.

Had the two gospels been somehow acknowledged as equally valid for the second time when Paul went up to Jerusalem to deliver the collection money, the history between Judaism and Christianity, which has been mostly antagonistic, to say the least, would have taken a very different course. When one voice becomes dominant at the cost of others, the community becomes the poorer. The two gospels in earliest Christianity should both have continued to exist.

Chapter 8

Conclusions and
Hermeneutical Ramifications

This book is an attempt at providing a coherent narrative of Paul's life focusing on what I regard as crucial events in his career as an "apostle" of Christ to the Gentiles. I have tried to retell the stories of the two gospels in early Christianity in Paul's time—i.e., the gospel of the circumcision and the gospel of the uncircumcision—as they unfolded through such landmark events as the Apostolic Council in Jerusalem, the Antioch Incident, the Galatian Incident, the Corinthian Incident, and Paul's last visit to Jerusalem.

In my reconstruction of the course of events I have highlighted Paul's unrelenting effort to defend his gospel and have characterized it as a struggle for inclusivity. I interpret this action as a practice of Paul's missiological principle to include Gentiles qua Gentiles in the community of God's people. It reflects a theological recognition that God accepts human beings just as they are. That is the quintessential meaning of the grace of God, as Paul understands it.[1] It was a struggle for Paul because such a theology/practice ran counter to a conventional soteriology held by the more influential Jewish Christians at that time. Paul was always put on the defensive and his struggle yielded varying degrees of success on different occasions, but overall he managed to hold his communities together under the umbrella of his inclusive gospel. In the meantime, however, the gap between the two gospels in early Christianity had grown bigger.

Having to defend his theological position against attacks from without had made Paul polemical in his arguments. As a result, while he included "others" (i.e., Gentiles), he alienated and was alienated by his own (i.e., his fellow Jewish Christians), who had a different theological position. This situation hurt Paul and he was determined to mend it. The collection project for the Jerusalem church is a symbol of Paul's attempt at reconciliation. It constitutes another phase of his struggle for inclusivity. This time it was to include the "other gospel," an act that would not have been possible without some theological accommodation on Paul's part. That is exactly what we found in what Paul said and did during the last few years of his life. He grew to a theological maturity that allowed him to accept and celebrate all people of God, be they *either Jew or Gentile*.

In fact, one of the most important observations we have made in this book is that Paul's theology, especially as it is articulated in soteriological terms, changed over the course of his life. It changed not haphazardly but as a result of the thoughtful reflections he had, mainly in retrospect, on the meaning of his struggle to defend his gospel against attacks from people who advocated a different kind of gospel. That is why there is a fundamentally existential dimension in Paul's theology, whatever stage of development it represents.

We noted that the change of Paul's soteriological horizon is most conspicuous in the contrast between his earlier position articulated in Galatians and his later stance reflected in Romans and Philippians. In the former, the gospel of the uncircumcision, according to which a human being is justified not by the works of the law but through faith/faithfulness (πίστις) in/of Jesus Christ, is the only valid way of salvation. In that case, only those who believe in this particular form of gospel could be saved. In the latter, Gentile Christians with the gospel of the uncircumcision, Jewish Christians with the gospel of the circumcision, and, perhaps more emphatically, *all* Israel are included in God's salvation.

This remarkably inclusive soteriological horizon is presented by Paul not in the form of dogma but in the language of faith and hope. Paul does not provide elaborate theological arguments for that. Instead, he sings a doxology that praises the mystery of God that saves God's people in God's terms beyond the dogmatic confines of human understanding of God's will:[2]

> O the depth of the riches and wisdom and knowledge of God! How unsearchable are his judgments and how inscrutable his ways!
>> "For who has known the mind of the Lord?
>>> Or who has been his counselor?"
>> "Or who has given a gift to him,
>>> to receive a gift in return?"
> For from him and through him and to him are all things. To him be the glory forever. Amen.
>
> (Rom. 11:33–36)

As this citation from the NRSV shows, Paul lived in too ancient a time to be aware of the problem of the gender-exclusive reference to God! That issue of gender exclusivity in biblical language had to wait almost two thousand years to be addressed and rendered more inclusive. Paul's main concern of inclusivity, however—especially his later, more mature soteriology inclusive of Jewish Christians and Gentile Christians on the one hand, and Christian Jews and non-Christian Jews on the other—was part of the current discussion in Second Temple Judaism and subsequently in early Christianity. There is no reason why this inclusive soteriology of Paul should have waited so long a time to be recognized and appreciated.

It is true that a particular hermeneutical lens in Christianity, especially in its Protestant branch, prevented certain aspects of Paul's theology from being recognized for a long time. Even the allegedly objective historical criticism was not able to completely remove this interpretive barrier. Now a new ethos in a new era—whether one calls it postmodernism, multiculturalism, or religiocultural pluralism—has opened a new hermeneutical horizon, against which conventional ideas, perspectives, and reading habits can and should be refocused. It is time that Christians carefully rethink how they see "others" who inhabit the same earth God created for all humanity. Moreover, it is important to recognize that the Bible contains materials that represent highly inclusive theological ideas. Such ideas may hitherto have been hidden from our eyes for various reasons, and it takes new reading strategies to be able to rediscover them. I hope I have shown one example of it in this book.

It is an irony that Christian soteriology presumably based on Paul's theology in Galatians and Romans generally has tended to claim a "universal validity" and become triumphalist and exclusivist as a result, refusing to see authenticity in any form of "other"-ness. We have seen in this book that a holistic understanding of Paul's theology does not necessarily support such an exclusivist soteriology. Therefore, the conventional, exclusivist Christian soteriology will have to be revised through careful historical reconstructions as well as existentially meaningful theological appropriations.

Paul's theology, which was situated in its own sociocultural location and embedded in its own historical particularities, will never be able to give a concrete and direct answer to such contemporary issues of our time as interfaith dialogue or religious pluralism. It can certainly shed light on them, however, by way of providing an example of an existentially anchored intellectual struggle concerning the fundamental issues of inclusivity in human religiosity. In this regard, Paul's unfolding theology of inclusivity still has much to contribute to our effort to remain faithful as Christians and at the same time become good citizens of the global village—citizens who are willing and able to see essential authenticity in others, as Paul saw a glimpse of it long ago. Thus, the struggle for inclusivity continues.

Notes

Introduction

1. One may argue that the Trinitarian doctrine of Christianity may disqualify Christianity as a monotheistic religion. I am not interested in ontological categorization. What I mean by monotheism here is the exclusive claim that one's deity is the only legitimate divine being. In that sense all the three branches of the Abrahamic religious tradition (i.e., Judaism, Christianity, and Islam) can be regarded as monotheistic.
2. In that context, I will highlight the *difference* between Galatians as an earlier letter of Paul and Romans as one of his last letters.
3. Here I accept the basic concept of F. C. Baur's thesis on the early Christian schism as generally correct, although I disagree with him with regard to how the schism developed and who represented which party.
4. The meaning of the term "conversion" in these cases will be discussed later in chapter 2.

Chapter 1: Particularism and Universalism in Mediterranean Antiquity

1. *The Oxford English Dictionary,* 2nd ed., edited by J. A. Simpson and E. S. C. Weiner (Oxford: Clarendon Press; New York: Oxford University Press, 1989), s.v. "universalism."
2. Simpson and Weiner, *The Oxford English Dictionary,* s.v. "universalist."
3. Julian Morgenstern, "Universalism and Particularism," in Isaac Landman, ed., *The Universal Jewish Encyclopedia.* Vol. 10 (New York: The Universal Jewish Encyclopedia, Inc., 1939), pp. 353–62; Geoffrey Wigoder, ed., *The Encyclopedia of Judaism* (N.Y.: Macmillan, 1989), s.v. "universalism and particularism"; Jacob Neusner, ed., *Dictionary of Judaism in the Biblical Period: 450 B.C.E. to 600 C.E.* 2 vols. (N.Y.: Macmillan, 1996) s.v. "universalism." Neusner defines universalism as a "term used to describe a more open attitude toward the gentile world on the part of Jews." Then he adds, "Although Ezra and Nehemiah show an exclusivistic attitude, others thought the community should be more outward looking and open to the surrounding culture."
4. Max L. Stackhouse, "Missions: Missionary Activity," in Mircea Eliade, ed., *Encyclopedia of Religion.* Vol. 9. New York: Macmillan, 1987. "Missionizing religions are religions that, impelled by a unique revelation or a great discovery about the nature of being, or a momentous social transformation and revitalization of purpose sparked by spiritual impulses, have generated a salvific metaphysical-moral vision that they believe to be of *universal* import for humanity" (italics mine).

5. *The Oxford English Dictionary,* s.v. "particularism."

6. Jon D. Levenson, "The Universal Horizon of Biblical Particularism," in *Ethnicity and the Bible,* Biblical Interpretation Series, vol. 19, ed. Mark G. Brett (Leiden: E. J. Brill, 1996), 143–69. This quotation is from p. 144.

7. The Greek word, βάρβαροι, is an onomatopoeia, mimicking those who only "babble" because they do not know how to speak Greek.

8. Plato, *Menexenus,* 245d. ἀλλ᾿ αὐτοὶ Ἕλληνες οὐ μειξοβάρβαροι οἰκοῦμεν ὅθεν καθαρὸν τὸ μῖσος ἐντέτηκε τῇ πόλει τῆς ἀλλοτρίας φύσεως (translation mine). An ambiguity exists in this sentence concerning the function of the genitive, τῆς ἀλλοτρίας φύσεως. It can be either objective genitive or subjective genitive for τὸ μῖσος.

9. Aristotle, *Politics,* I.1.1252b.9. Similar derogatory statements about foreigners (barbarians) are found in III.9.1285a.20; VII.8.1329a.26; VII.9.1330a.29, etc.

10. Aeschylus, *Eum.* 40; Plato, *Resp.* 427c; Strabo, *Geogr.* 9.3.6.

11. Diogenes Laertius, VI.63. ἐρωτηθεὶς πόθεν εἴη, κοσμοπολίτης ἔφη.

12. Diogenes Laertius, VI.72. μόνην τε ὀρθὴν πολιτείαν εἶναι τὴν ἐν κόσμῳ.

13. Plutarch, *Alex. fort.,* I.6 (329A).

14. Ibid., I.6 (329B).

15. Strabo, *Geogr.,* 1.4.9.

16. William Tarn, *Alexander the Great,* vol. 2 (Cambridge: Cambridge University Press, 1948), 399–49. For a counterargument, see E. Badian, "Alexander the Great and the Unity of Mankind," *Historia* 7 (1958): 425–44.

17. For example, Gen. 12:3, which belongs to the Yahwist (J) source, seems to show a universalistic tendency. Rabbinic literature indeed used this passage for universalistic interpretation of the Scripture. However, there is a problem of ambiguity of the critical term נברכו(ו). If it is taken as reflexive, the entire verse means that the well-being of all the nations will depend on how they treat the descendants of Abraham, which is highly particularistic. Cf. Claus Westermann, *Genesis 12–36: A Commentary,* trans. J. Scullion (Minneapolis: Augsburg, 1985), 151–52.

18. Shaye J. D. Cohen says, "According to an old joke, there are two kinds of people in the world: those who divide the world into two kinds of people, and those who do not. Jews are in the former category: like numerous other groups, both ancient and modern, Jews see the world in bipolar terms: Jews versus gentiles, 'us' versus 'them'" (Shaye J. D. Cohen, *The Beginnings of Jewishness: Boundaries, Varieties, Uncertainties* [Berkeley, Calif.: University of California Press, 1999], 1).

19. Henry Jackson et al., in speaking of "the major expansion of Israel's faith" by Ezekiel and Deutero-Isaiah during the exile, say: "The *old narrow provincialism* that had been expressed in reverence for the Jerusalem sanctuary gave way to a *broader* and more sublime interpretation of Yahweh's concern for all people" (italics mine) (Henry Jackson et al., *People of the Covenant,* 4th ed. [London: Oxford University Press, 1996], 428).

20. Here, with regard to Deutero-Isaiah, Bernhard Anderson says, "But the Exile also awakened a *new world-consciousness.* Israel's faith was enlarged by the *vision of new horizons* that had never been seen so clearly before, not even in the cosmopolitan age of Solomon. Israel realized that they must look beyond their own circumscribed community to the whole civilized world if they would behold the glory and majesty of Yahweh's purpose in history" (italics mine) (Bernhard W. Anderson, *Understanding the Old Testament,* 4th ed. [Englewood Cliffs, N.J.: Prentice-Hall, 1986], 468).

21. Isaiah 49:6b: וּנְתַתִּיךָ לְאוֹר גּוֹיִם לִהְיוֹת יְשׁוּעָתִי עַד־קְצֵה הָאָרֶץ׃

22. An even more universalistic passage is found in Isa. 19:16–25, in which Egypt and Assyria are identified as God's own people. However, this remarkable passage has been regarded by the majority of scholars as a later interpolation by a post-exilic redactor. See John F. A. Sawyer, "'Blessed Be My People Egypt (Isaiah 19.25)': The Context and Meaning of a Remarkable Passage," in *A Word in Season: Essays in Honour of William McKane*, ed. James D. Martin and Philip R. Davies, JSOT Supplement Series 42 (Sheffield: JSOT Press, 1986), 57–71; see esp. 58–59. Some scholars even date this passage to the Seleucid-Ptolemaic period in Jewish history: e.g., Harry M. Orlinsky, "Nationalism-Universalism and Internationalism in Ancient Israel," in *Translating and Understanding the Old Testament: Essays in Honor of Herbert Gordon May*, ed. H. T. Frank and W. L. Reed (Nashville: Abingdon, 1970), 206–236; see especially 223.

23. Anderson, *Understanding the Old Testament*, 485–86. However, by way of caution Anderson adds, "There is a broad universality in Second Isaiah's message, and yet never does this prophet surrender the conviction that Israel occupies a special place in Yahweh's historical plan" (485).

24. Anderson, *Understanding the Old Testament*, 516.

25. Norman K. Gottwald, *The Hebrew Bible: A Socio-Literary Introduction* (Philadelphia: Fortress Press, 1985), 428–29.

26. Even though Jonah is the protagonist, he is not a hero but an antihero throughout the story.

27. וַיִּירְאוּ and וַיִּזְבְּחוּ־זֶבַח in v. 16 are typical words of worship.

28. Hans Walter Wolff, *Obadiah and Jonah: A Commentary*, trans. M. Kohl (Minneapolis: Augsburg, 1986), 78–80 and 128–29.

29. Anderson, *Understanding the Old Testament*, 604–605.

30. In fact, this particular tension is just a part of the larger picture of the diversity and variety of Second Temple Judaism. See Anderson, *Understanding the Old Testament*, 605.

31. For the diversity of opinion of the Tannaitic rabbis concerning the salvation of Gentiles, see E. P. Sanders, *Paul and Palestinian Judaism* (Minneapolis: Fortress, 1977), 206–212. See also Alan F. Segal, "Universalism in Judaism and Christianity," in *Paul in His Hellenistic Context*, ed. Troels Engberg-Pedersen (Minneapolis: Fortress Press, 1995), 1–29. Here Segal correctly argues that both Judaism and Christianity had complicated internal debates including both sides of the issue of particularism and universalism, and he cites a number of Jewish documents for different theological positions during Second Temple Judaism.

32. Translation from James H. Charlesworth, ed., *The Old Testament Pseudepigrapha*, vol. 2 (New York: Doubleday, 1985), 87.

33. Segal, "Universalism in Judaism and Christianity," 10–11. See also idem, *Paul the Convert: The Apostolate and Apostasy of Saul the Pharisee* (New Haven, Conn.: Yale University Press, 1990), 196.

34. Segal, "Universalism in Judaism and Christianity," 10.

35. Segal, "Universalism in Judaism and Christianity," 11.

36. *B. Shabbath* 31a. Translation is taken from I. Epstein, ed., *Hebrew-English Edition of the Babylonian Talmud: Shabbath*, vol. 1 (London: The Soncino Press, 1972). The full text of what Hillel said is as follows:

דעלך סני לחברך לא תעביד
זו היא כל התנוה כולה ואידך פירושה הוא
זיל גמור

37. *Makkot* 2.3.

38. *Jubilees* 22:16, "Separate yourself from the nations and eat not with them. . . . For their works are unclean and all their ways are a pollution and an abomination and an uncleanness."
39. The citation is from Sanders, *Paul and Palestinian Judaism*, 150.
40. *Midrash Devarim Rabbah* 2.24. Quotation from *Midrash Rabbah: Deuteronomy*, ed. H. Freedman and Maurice Simon, trans. J. Rabbinowitz (London: Soncino Press, 1939), 52.
41. *T. Sanh.* 13:2; English translation from *The Tosefta Translated from the Hebrew*, vol. 4, ed. Jacob Neusner (New York: KTAV Publishing House, 1977–86), 238.
42. *B. Baba Bathra* 10b; English translation from *Hebrew-English Edition of the Babylonian Talmud: Baba Bathra*, ed. I. Epstein (London: The Soncino Press, 1976).
43. *B. Sanh.* 59a.
44. *B. B. Qam.* 38a.
45. According to Segal, "The Noahide Commandments function like a concept of natural law, which any just person can be expected to follow by observation and reason. In Christian theological language, it is available by God's grace to all humanity." Segal also rightly recognizes that the Noahide Commandments include monotheism and, "sometimes, recognition that the Lord, the God of Israel, is the one true God" (Segal, *Paul the Convert*, 195; Idem, "Universalism in Judaism and Christianity," 9). In other words, the phrase "any just person" means the one who at least embraced the monotheism of Judaism, just as, in traditional Christian theology, grace is extended not to "all humanity" but only to those who embraced the belief in Jesus Christ.
46. Segal, "Universalism in Judaism and Christianity," 9.
47. In fact, one of the seven commandments of the Noachian Law was a prohibition of idolatry. Unlike the other six commandments, which are not related to religious practice, this monotheistic commandment almost by default would severely limit the number of the Gentiles who could be regarded as having fulfilled the Noachian Law, since most Gentiles were polytheistic. Therefore, strictly speaking, this commandment could be fulfilled by those Gentiles who worship no other god than the only true God Yahweh. In other words, Gentiles may not have to convert to Judaism by going through circumcision but they still have to embrace the monotheistic practice of the Jewish religion in order to be saved. So one may have to say the Noachian Law is universalistic in a slightly modified sense of the word. See Heikki Räisänen, *Marcion, Muhammad, and the Mahatma: Exegetical Perspectives on the Encounter of Cultures and Faiths* (London: SCM Press, 1997), 34.

Chapter 2: The Beginning of Early Christianity

1. It is true that to use the word "Christianity" for the community of the followers of Jesus prior to their separation from Judaism is anachronism. I will use the term "early Christianity" in this book rather comprehensively to include the Jesus movement within Judaism as well as the Hellenistic Christian communities. For further discussion on this subject see James D. Dunn, *The Acts of the Apostles* (London: Epworth Press, 1996), 1–2.
2. It is a question whether John distinguishes the resurrection from ascension or not. John 20:17 does imply that Jesus will take another step to go to his father. However, as John 14:1–14 shows, the Johannine language of coming and going is highly metaphoric.
3. For an interpretation of the different treatments of the whereabouts of the resurrected Jesus in the Synoptic Gospels, see Eung Chun Park, "The ΑΠΟΥΣΙΑ of Jesus in the Synoptic Resurrection Traditions," in *Antiquity and Humanity: Essays on Ancient Religion and Philosophy Presented to Hans Dieter Betz on His 70th*

Birthday, ed. Adela Yarbro Collins and Margaret M. Mitchell (Tübingen: Mohr Siebeck, 2001), 121–35.

4. *Gos. Pet.* ix (translation mine).

5. For examples of two opposing views on the historicity of the ascension of Jesus in Acts see I. Howard Marshall, *The Acts of the Apostles* (Downers Grove, Ill.: InterVarsity Press, 1980), 59–60; and Gerd Lüdemann, *Early Christianity according to the Traditions in Acts* (London: SCM, 1989), 29–31.

6. Cf. Elisabeth Schüssler Fiorenza, *In Memory of Her: A Feminist Theological Reconstruction of Christian Origins*, 10th anniversary ed. (New York: Crossroad, 1994), 139. Here Fiorenza conjectures that the Galilean male disciples of Jesus fled back to Galilee after Jesus' arrest, while the women followers remained in Jerusalem through the crucifixion and later became convinced of the vindication of Jesus by God. According to Fiorenza's surmise, some of these women remained in Jerusalem and some of them went back to Galilee and delivered the good news of Jesus' resurrection to the male disciples there, thus becoming the first pioneers of the post-Easter Jesus movement in Galilee.

7. If we accept the scholarly consensus that John 21 is a later addition by a redactor, it is fascinating to observe that the original Johannine tradition of the resurrection of Jesus (chap. 20) implies that the appearance of the resurrected Jesus happens in Jerusalem whereas the later redactional addition (chap. 21) says Jesus appears to some of his disciples on the shore of the sea of Tiberias, which is in Galilee (John 21:1). Is the later redactor trying to harmonize the Jerusalem tradition of Luke and the Galilee tradition of Mark and Matthew?

8. For the possibility of parallel existence of a Galilean Church and a Jerusalem Church, see Ernst Lohmeyer, *Galiläa und Jerusalem* (Göttingen: Vandenhoeck and Ruprecht, 1936); and Rudolph Bultmann, *Theology of the New Testament* (New York: Charles Scribner's Sons, 1951), 52.

9. Cf. Michael Goulder's comment: "[S]o it is likely that *Peter, James and John*, the sons of Zebedee, ran the Jerusalem church at first, while the *Nine* supervised things in Galilee" (italics his). This is an interesting suggestion, but there is no evidence for it (Michael Goulder, *St. Paul versus St. Peter: A Tale of Two Missions* [Louisville, Ky.: Westminster John Knox, 1994], 8).

10. Ernst Käsemann presupposes that the disciples went back to Galilee after the crucifixion. Then he conjectures that, because of the expectation of an imminent parousia of Jesus, these fugitive disciples later returned to Jerusalem, which is the place the Jewish people already expected the epiphany of the Messiah (Ernst Käsemann, *New Testament Questions of Today* [Philadelphia: Fortress Press, 1979], 114).

11. C. K. Barrett uses the word "nationalist" to mean the same. I use the word "particularist" in order to put it in the context of the history of the tension between particularism and universalism in Judaism (C. K. Barrett, *The Acts of the Apostles*, vol. 1 [Edinburgh: T. & T. Clark, 1994], 76).

12. F. C. Baur, *Paul the Apostle of Jesus Christ, His Life and Work, His Epistles and His Doctrine: A Contribution to a Critical History of Primitive Christianity*, 2nd ed., trans. E. Zeller (London: Williams and Norgate, 1876).

13. Baur uses the term "deacon" for those seven leaders of the Hellenists, but the text of Acts 6:5–6 does not say they are deacons (Baur, *Paul the Apostle*, 41). In fact, the term διάκονος is never used in Acts. According to Bultmann, "For those seven were not 'deacons' but were, as their Greek names (6:5) show, representatives of the Hellenistic party. What is told of Stephen, and later of Philip, also indicates that their office was by no means serving table, but that they were proclaimers of the word" (Bultmann, *Theology*, vol. 1, 56).

14. Baur, *Paul the Apostle*, 39.

15. The division of factionalism in the Jerusalem church into the Hellenists and the Hebrews has been widely accepted by scholars since Baur. See, for example, Bultmann, *Theology*, vol. 1, 55–56; and Günther Bornkamm, "The History of the Origin of the So-called Second Letter to the Corinthians," *NTS* 8 (1962): 13–14. See also Hans Conzelmann, *A Commentary on the Acts of the Apostles*, Hermeneia (Philadelphia: Fortress Press, 1987), 45; Ernst Haenchen, *The Acts of the Apostles: A Commentary* (Oxford: Basil Blackwell, 1971), 264–65; James D. Dunn, *The Partings of the Ways: Between Christianity and Judaism and their Significance for the Character of Christianity* (London: SCM, 1991), 60–64; and Schuyler Brown, *The Origins of Christianity: A Historical Introduction to the New Testament* (New York: Oxford University Press, 1984), 96–97. Note that Craig C. Hill, *Hellenists and Hebrews: Reappraising Division within the Earliest Church* (Minneapolis: Fortress Press, 1992), 5–17; and Ben Witherington III, *The Acts of the Apostles: A Socio-Rhetorical Commentary* (Grand Rapids: William B. Eerdmans Publishing Company, 1998), 242–47, challenge this view, arguing for a more complex situation in the Jerusalem church.
16. Hengel, *Acts and the History of Earliest Christianity* (London: SCM, 1979), 71.
17. John Knox, *Chapters in a Life of Paul*, rev. and ed. D. R. A. Hare (Macon, Ga.: Mercer University Press, 1987), 3–5.
18. Examples of the former are Hengel, *Acts and the History of Earliest Christianity*; I. Howard Marshall, *Luke: Historian and Theologian* (London: The Paternoster Press, 1970); Rainer Riesner, *Paul's Early Period: Chronology, Mission Strategy, Theology* (Grand Rapids: Eerdmans, 1998). For the latter see Knox, *Chapters in a Life of Paul*; Gerd Lüdemann, *Paul: Apostle to the Gentiles: Studies in Chronology* (London: SCM, 1984). For a middle position see Robert Jewett, *A Chronology of Paul's Life* (Philadelphia: Fortress Press, 1979).
19. Emphasizing the continuity between "before" and "after" with regard to "Paul's experience on the Damascus Road," Krister Stendahl argues that it is not a conversion so much as a prophetic call that Paul went through. What he denies here is the use of the term conversion in the sense of "change of religion," which is obviously not what it is about. But if we use the term more broadly as meaning "change of mind," it can very well be applied to Paul's experience (Krister Stendahl, *Paul among Jews and Gentiles* [Philadelphia: Fortress Press, 1976], 7).
20. Thucydides, *Hist.* 1.22. Concerning the speeches in his book, Thucydides here admits the difficulty of recalling the actual speeches accurately and says that in composing the speeches he only tries to reproduce the *general sense* of what was actually said (ἐγγύτατα τῆς ξυμπάσης γνώμης τῶν ἀληθῶς λεχθέντων) based upon what he thinks was necessary (τὰ δέοντα) for the speakers to have said. We do not know whether Luke was aware of this Thucydidean tradition or not. Nor do we know if he had a similar sense of methodological modesty. Luke's preface (Luke 1:1–4), especially his language in vv. 3–4, seems to reveal that he is more confident than Thucydides was about the accuracy of what he writes in his book.
21. Knox, *Chapters in a Life of Paul*, 20.
22. Strabo, in *The Geography of Strabo*, ed. H. L. Jones, Loeb Classical Library, vol. 6 (Cambridge, Mass.: Harvard University Press, 1924), 347.
23. Sherman E. Johnson, *Paul the Apostle and His Cities* (Wilmington, Del.: Michael Glazier, Inc., 1987), 29.
24. Knox, *Chapters in a Life of Paul*, 21.
25. Riesner, *Paul's Early Period*, 154. See also Jerome Murphy-O'Connor, *Paul: A Critical Life* (Oxford: Clarendon Press, 1996), 59. Based upon his reconstruction of Paul's chronology, Murphy-O'Connor also argues that Paul's acquaintance with Gamaliel in Jerusalem is plausible.

26. Even though this passage has traditionally been interpreted as meaning that Simeon, Gamaliel, and Simeon are direct descendants from Hillel, the Talmudic text itself does not explicitly say that they are. However, whether or not Gamaliel is indeed Hillel's grandson, as the traditional interpretation has it, what remains true is that he is the heir of the scholarly tradition of Hillel. Cf. Neusner, *The Rabbinic Traditions about the Pharisees before 70*, vol. 1, South Florida Studies in the History of Judaism 201 (Atlanta: Scholars Press, 1999), 15 and 294–95. Here Neusner is highly skeptical about the alleged family connection between Hillel and Gamaliel.

27. For stories of Hillel and Shammai and those of Gamaliel, see Judah Nadich, *The Legends of the Rabbis*, vol. 1 (London: Jason Aronson, 1983), 200–11 and 238–43; as for Hillel's attitude toward Gentiles, see Yitzhak Buxbaum, *The Life and Teaching of Hillel* (Northvale, N.J.: Jason Aronson, Inc., 1994), 72–75.

28. Hengel, *Acts and the History of Earliest Christianity*, 73.

29. According to Matt. 23:15, the scribes and the Pharisees were actively seeking proselytes. The historicity of this passage has been debated. For a further discussion see W. D. Davies and D. C. Allison, *A Critical and Exegetical Commentary on the Gospel of Saint Matthew*, vol. 3 (Edinburgh: T. & T. Clark, 1997), 287–89.

30. H. J. Schoeps points out, "It is to be supposed that Saul the Pharisee of the Diaspora was such a missionary before his conversion" (H. J. Schoeps, *Paul: The Theology of the Apostle in the Light of Jewish Religious History*, trans. H. Knight [London: Lutterworth Press, 1961], 219); likewise F. F. Bruce says, "But if Paul had engaged in proselytization among Gentiles before his conversion, he would certainly have preached circumcision then: such a zealot for the tradition would not have viewed circumcision as optional" (F. F. Bruce, *The Epistle of Paul to the Galatians: A Commentary on the Greek Text* [Exeter: Paternoster Press, 1982], 236).

31. The traditional assumption of the existence of Jewish mission in the first century C.E. has been seriously challenged. See Martin Goodman, *Mission and Conversion* (Oxford: Clarendon Press, 1994), 60–90, in which Goodman argues that there is very little evidence for the universal proselytizing mission in Judaism before 100 C.E. See also idem, "Jewish Proselytizing in the First Century," in *The Jews among Pagans and Christians in the Roman Empire*, ed. J. Lieu et al. (London: Routledge, 1992), 53–78. According to Scot McKnight, "Judaism never developed a clear mission to the Gentiles that had as its goal the conversion of the world. Further, . . . there is no evidence that could lead to the conclusion that Judaism was a 'missionary religion' in the sense of aggressive attempts to convert Gentiles or in the sense of self-identity" (Scot McKnight, *A Light among the Gentiles* [Minneapolis: Fortress, 1991], 116–17).

32. Stendahl, *Paul among Jews and Gentiles*, 7–23. Stendahl says Paul's experience was not a conversion but a call to a specific task.

33. Lüdemann, *Early Christianity according to the Traditions in Acts*, 114. Lüdemann finds the "Easter language" both in 1 Cor. 9:1 and 1 Cor. 15:8.

34. Baur maintains, "And as together with his calling to the office of an Apostle he claimed to have received also a distinct commission to proclaim the Gospel to the Gentiles, so the whole question as to the participation of the Gentiles in the Messianic Salvation, which was a cause of so bitter dispute between the Apostle and the Jewish Christians, rests also on the truth and reality of the visionary appearance by which the Apostle believed himself to have been called" (Baur, *Paul the Apostle*, 78).

35. A popular notion of what happened to Paul when he saw the vision of Jesus is that it was his "conversion" from one religion to another, that is, from Judaism to Christianity. Considering that the separation between Judaism and Christianity did not occur until much later, this way of understanding Paul's vision

experience is anachronistic and plainly wrong. Both prior and subsequent to this experience, Paul always remained a bona fide proud, faithful, and patriotic Jew. Obviously, this vision experience caused him to change his perspective on Jesus, and it gave him a strong sense of call to be an "apostle" to Gentiles. It is in this sense of "change of mind" that I use the term "conversion" for Paul in this book. See Stendahl, *Paul among Jews and Gentiles,* 7–23.

36. Dunn, *Acts,* 134, also has the title, "The Conversion of Peter and the Acceptance of Cornelius" for Acts 10:1–48. Just like Paul in Acts 9, Peter in Acts 10 also had a vision experience, which caused a significant change in his mind. Since Peter was already a follower of Jesus at the time of this vision experience, however, it is not usually called a "conversion" experience. It goes without saying that, again just like Paul, Peter never ceased being a faithful Jew throughout his life. No change of religions ever happened to him. Nevertheless, the vision experience of Peter in the narrative world of Acts 10 does mark a paradigm shift in his understanding of the purity law, and it is in that sense that I apply the term "conversion" to Peter in this book.

37. Again, the use of the term "Christian" is anachronistic, but here I use the term as a reference to the Jews who believed Jesus as the Messiah.

38. *Pace* Baur, who famously argued that Peter and Paul were the two rival leaders of the two competing factions in early Christianity. See also Goulder, *St. Paul versus St. Peter,* 1–7 and 181–89.

39. In the case of Jonah it is clearly stated as דְּבַר־יְהוָה (Jonah 1:1). In Peter's story it is just a φωνή (Acts 10:13), and it refers to God in the third person singular in 10:15b, which implies that it is an angelic voice communicating a message of God.

40. Dunn, *Acts,* 137, says, "He refuses and implicitly rebukes the heavenly visitation."

41. For the importance of the purity law in Second Temple Judaism, see Dunn, *The Partings of the Ways,* 38–44.

42. B. *Baba Mezia,* 596, in *Hebrew-English Edition of the Babylonian Talmud: Baba Mezia,* ed. I. Epstein (London: Soncino Press, 1971).

43. In fact, the change of leadership in the Jerusalem church from Peter to James is not explicitly narrated in Acts. It is only by inference from chapters 12, 15, and 21 of Acts that we come to know that it happened. It is interesting that Eusebius has a quotation from the *Hypotyposes* of Clement of Alexandria that says Peter, James, and John appointed James the Just (Ἰάκωβον τὸν δίκαιον) as bishop (ἐπίσκοπον) of Jerusalem after the ascension of the Savior (*Hist. Eccl.* 2.1.2), as if James had been the leader of the Jerusalem church from the very beginning. This tradition, whatever its ultimate origin was, could be an attempt to legitimize the period of the leadership of James in Jerusalem by connecting it with the original apostles.

Chapter 3: The Apostolic Council in Jerusalem

1. In fact, the text does not contain the words οἱ Ἑλληνισταί, but the accounts in chaps. 7–8 make it sufficiently clear that the Hellenists were the ones that were persecuted. See Raymond Brown and John Meier, *Antioch and Rome: New Testament Cradles of Catholic Christianity* (London: Geoffrey Chapman, 1983), 32–33.

2. According to Josephus, *Ant.* 12.119–24, Seleucus Nicator (reigned 312–281 B.C.E.), the founder of the city of Antioch, granted the Jews citizenship and equal privileges with the Macedonians and the Greeks. These privileges continued to the times of Josephus. When the people of Alexandria and Antioch petitioned that the privileges of citizenship be taken away from the Jews in their cities, Vespasian and Titus did not grant their wishes and let the Jews maintain the privileges.

3. Jerome Murphy-O'Connor says, "At this stage in the history of the church it was taken for granted by all including Paul, that salvation was related to the chosen people, who worshipped the one God, and to whom he had sent his Messiah. The salvation question as far as Gentiles were concerned was: how can they be integrated into God's messianic people?" (Murphy-O'Connor, *Paul*, 134). This could be an overstatement. Not every Jew at that time would agree that salvation is limited to the chosen people.

4. See n. 31 in chap. 2.

5. There is a textual problem for the word Ἑλληνιστάς in Acts 11:20. A few manuscripts have a variant reading Ἕλληνας instead, for which neither external nor internal evidence is very strong. It is probably a scribal effort to substitute a less ambiguous word (Ἕλληνας) for a potentially confusing one (Ἑλληνιστάς). For a discussion on this textual problem see Bruce Metzger, *A Textual Commentary on the Greek New Testament* (New York: United Bible Society, 1971), 388. The word Ἑλληνιστής derived from Ἑλληνίζω, which means "speak Greek" (Plato, *Meno* 82b) or "speak or write pure Greek" (Aristotle, *Rhetoric* 1407a 19), and therefore it means "one who uses the Greek language" [Henry George Liddell & Robert Scott, eds., *A Greek-English Lexicon,* 9th ed. (Oxford: Clarendon Press, 1968]). Even though in Acts 6:1 and 9:29 its plural form Ἑλληνισταί specifically means "Greek-speaking Jews," its semantic range should not be confined to one ethnic group. Therefore, both Ἑλληνισταί and Ἕλληνες could mean "Greek speakers" in general. As for Acts 11:20, the context gives us a hint that the word, whether Ἑλληνιστάς or Ἕλληνας, means "Gentiles," because it is used in contrast to Ἰουδαίοις (Jews) in Acts 11:19.

6. In the passage about the founding of the Antioch church (Acts 11:19–30), the word ἐκκλησία appears only in v. 26.

7. Witherington, *Acts*, 371.

8. Wayne Meeks and Robert Wilken, *Jews and Christians in Antioch in the First Four Centuries of the Common Era*, SBL Sources for Biblical Study 13 (Missoula, Mont.: Scholars Press, 1978), 13–15; and Brown and Meier, *Antioch and Rome*, 33. See especially the excursus on Χριστιανοί in Conzelmann, *Acts*, 88–89.

9. For a summary of debate on the historicity of this episode see Brown and Meier, 33–34.

10. Because Paul does not say he was brought to Antioch by Barnabas, Conzelmann says Luke may have inferred Barnabas's journey to Tarsus from his presence in Antioch and from his subsequent cooperation with Paul (Conzelmann, *Acts*, 88).

11. In Acts Paul always goes to the Jews first and then to the Gentiles only when his gospel is rejected by the Jews. In contrast, Paul himself says he was called by God to preach the gospel to the Gentiles from the very beginning. The least we can say is Paul must have focused on Gentile mission throughout his life as a Christian but without necessarily excluding Jews as his audience.

12. The text does not say whether or not they were from Jerusalem. However, the same soteriological stance of the Pharisaic believers in the Jerusalem Church in Acts 15:5 makes it highly plausible that the individuals mentioned in Acts 15:1 came from the Jerusalem church. It is possible that Luke intentionally changed the reference of their provenance from Jerusalem, which he found in his source, to Judea in order to avoid the impression that the Jerusalem Church is responsible for the turmoil in Antioch. See Conzelmann, *Acts*, 115; and Haenchen, *Acts*, 442–43.

13. Even though this episode is narrated only in Acts, it has a high degree of probability as a historical event because it is the immediate cause for the Apostolic Council in Jerusalem, which can be firmly established as historical.

14. Prior to the destruction of the temple of Jerusalem, proselytes were required to go through the rite of circumcision, immersion, and offering of a sacrifice. After

the destruction of the temple, Johanan b. Zakkai instituted that a proselyte-sacrifice was no longer required. Thus only circumcision and immersion remained. For more information see Cecil Bezalel Roth and Geoffrey Wigoder, eds., *Encyclopedia Judaica* (Jerusalem: Keter Publishing House; New York: The Macmillan Co., 1972), s.v. "proselyte."

15. Witherington says, "This extreme view, which not merely requires circumcision but sees it as necessary for salvation, is precisely what we find Paul combating in Galatians . . . and thus there is good reason to think it is this same very conservative Jewish Christian faction that not only came to Antioch but proceeded on to Paul's newly founded churches in Galatia to spread their own message. Presumably they are also the same as the false brothers who debated this issue in Jerusalem" (Witherington, *Acts*, 450).

16. The title "Apostolic Council" may not be an appropriate one, because the controversy was mainly between the "Pharisaic" Jewish Christians in Jerusalem (Acts 15:5) and the delegates from the Antioch church, and neither party was "apostolic" in the traditional sense of the word. Also, the chair, James the Lord's brother, was not an apostle, either. The only apostles who were specifically mentioned as present there are Peter and John (Gal. 2:9), whom Paul calls the "pillars" (στῦλοι), not "apostles." In fact, long before this meeting took place, most apostles had left Jerusalem (Gal. 1:19). However, in the absence of a more adequate designation, I will continue to use the phrase "the Apostolic Council in Jerusalem" in this book.

17. Hill, *Hellenists and Hebrews*, 116–17. Here Hill correctly argues that the Jerusalem Council–Antioch Incident sequence best fits with Paul's narrative in Gal. 2 and Luke's report about the split between Paul and Barnabas in Acts 15:36–41.

18. For a comparison between the two accounts, see Haenchen, *Acts*, 462–68.

19. Hans Dieter Betz, *Galatians: A Commentary on Paul's Letter to the Churches in Galatia*, Hermeneia (Philadelphia: Fortress Press, 1979), 81.

20. James D. Dunn, *Jesus, Paul, and the Law: Studies in Mark and Galatians* (Louisville, Ky.: Westminster John Knox, 1990), 119.

21. Gerd Lüdemann, *Opposition to Paul in Jewish Christianity* (Minneapolis: Fortress, 1989), 52.

22. Murphy-O'Connor, *Paul*, 137.

23. There is a minor textual problem in Gal. 2:5. Some manuscripts (D* b) and patristic citations (the Latin versions of Irenaeus and Tertullian) omit οἷς οὐδέ, making the sentence mean that Paul, Barnabas, and Titus did yield to the demand of the circumcision party. This variant reading, mostly Western, is not well represented in terms of external evidence. It seems to be a scribal attempt at finding an analogue to the circumcision of Timothy (Acts 16:3). See Metzger, *A Textual Commentary*, 591–92.

24. According to H. D. Betz, "He seems to have two events in mind: one event included 'them' (αὐτοῖς), whoever they may have been; at another occasion he met 'separately' (κατ' ἰδίαν) with the 'men of reputation' (οἱ δοκοῦντες), that is, the 'pillars' (οἱ στῦλοι), James, Cephas, and John (cf. 2:9)" (Betz, *Galatians*, 86).

25. Acts is more explicit about the moderatorial role James played at the Apostolic Council (esp. Acts 15:13, 19). The verb κρίνω in Acts 15:19 suggests that James has the authority to make the final deliberation, and the pronoun ἐγώ in the same sentence highlights the ruling prerogative of James as the chair of the council. See Witherington, *Acts*, 457 and 467.

26. The theological position of the Pharisaic believers is clearly stated in Acts 15:5, but that of the Antioch delegation is not mentioned in Acts. It is however sufficiently implied in the context.

27. Interestingly, according to Acts, it is Peter not Paul who articulates the theology of salvation by grace (Acts 15:11) for the first time.

28. Haenchen, *Acts*, 468; and Conzelmann, *Acts*, 119. In contrast, Witherington affirms the historicity of the Apostolic Decree (Witherington, *Acts*, 467–68).

29. *Pace* J. Louis Martyn, who says, "In these parallel clauses, then, Paul in no way suggests that there are two gospels. There are, rather, two missions in which the one gospel is making its way into the whole of the cosmos" (J. Louis Martyn, *Galatians: A New Translation with Introduction and Commentary*, Anchor Bible 33A [New York: Doubleday, 1997], 202). It is true that Gal. 2:7 talks about two mission fields, but it is very implausible that the gospel as Paul came to define it in Galatians was agreed upon as "the one gospel" by the Pharisaic Jewish Christians at the Jerusalem Council. What is more likely is that the gospel of the Antioch delegates was sanctioned as equally valid with the then-uncontested gospel of the Jerusalem church. In that regard the expression of Gal. 2:7, which does mention two different gospels, seems to reflect the language of the original agreement of the Jerusalem Council. For a similar argument for the Council's sanctioning of two gospels, see Betz, who says, "The division of labor was made possible by the concept of two gospels, the 'gospel of the uncircumcision' and the 'gospel of the circumcision' (2:7), held together by the one God who works the salvation of mankind through both (2:8)" (Betz, *Galatians*, 82).

30. The term "circumcision," just like its parallel "Gentiles" in this verse, is used as an ethnographic reference. See Lüdemann, *Opposition to Paul*, 37.

31. It is interesting that in Gal. 2:8 Paul speaks explicitly about the apostolate of circumcision (ἀποστολὴν τῆς περιτομῆς) given to Peter, but he is careful not to mention the word "apostolate" with regard to his own commission. It is because his "apostleship" was never approved by the Apostolic Council in Jerusalem. Paul still claims that he is an apostle in the epistolary prescript (Gal. 1:1), but not in the section that narrates the decisions of the Apostolic Council in Jerusalem! This caution of Paul is understandable because the very question of his apostleship was a point of debate in the polemical situation of Galatians, even though it was not even brought up at the Apostolic Council in Jerusalem.

32. This aspect of the agreement is more explicitly reported by Paul in Gal. 2 than by Luke in Acts 15.

33. For a slightly lower appraisal of this concession see C. K. Barrett, "Paul: Councils and Controversies," in *Conflicts and Challenges in Early Christianity*, ed. Donald A. Hagner (Harrisburg, Pa.: Trinity Press International, 1999), 60. Here he says, "This was an agreement, and as such to be welcomed; but it is evident that it was essentially an agreement to differ, a compromise. . . . This was better than nothing, but it was by no means a wholehearted acceptance of one gospel (cf. Gal. 1:6) intended for the whole world." Obviously, Barrett is too Pauline to regard the "compromise" of the Apostolic Council in Jerusalem as a truly meaningful achievement.

34. Quintilian, *Inst.*, 4.2.83, "Namque ne iis quidem accedo qui semper eo putant ordine quo quid actum sit esse narrandum, sed eo malo narrare quo expedit." (For I do not agree with those who think that one should always narrate events in the order that they happened; instead, I prefer narrating them in the order that would be most expedient.—translation mine.)

35. For a recent discussion on this issue see Hill, *Hellenists and Hebrews*, 115–22. See also Murphy-O'Connor, *Paul*, 132.

36. C. K. Barrett, "Paul: Councils and Controversies," 44. Here, the ambiguities of the "compromise" at the Apostolic Council in Jerusalem are expressed by the following questions: "Was Paul an apostle or not? Are there two gospels? If Paul's gospel is true, the whole gospel is for the whole world; who has the right to say

Jews only, or Gentiles only? . . . If Jews were won by their gospel and Gentiles by theirs, how were Jewish converts to be related to Gentile converts?"

37. For the discussion of this inscription and its implications for Pauline chronology see Jerome Murphy-O'Connor, *St. Paul's Corinth: Text and Archaeology* (Collegeville, Minn.: Liturgical Press, 1983), 141–52.

38. Both the Apostolic Council in Jerusalem and the Antioch Incident are usually dated in the late 40s. See James Dunn, *Jesus, Paul, and the Law: Studies in Mark and Galatians* (Louisville, Ky.: Westminster/John Knox, 1990), 129–74.

39. Thucydides, *Hist.* I.22.1.

40. First Corinthians 11:17–34 indicates that the Lord's Supper (κυριακὸν δεῖπνον) was a full meal integrated into the worship in Pauline churches. For a discussion of the sociocultural implications of this practice see Gerd Theissen, *The Social Setting of Pauline Christianity: Essays on Corinth* (Philadelphia: Fortress Press, 1982), 145–68.

41. For a list of passages in Jewish literature that present Gentiles as unclean, see Dunn, *Jesus, Paul, and the Law*, 142–43. Also, for a discussion of the Jewish scruples about the regulations of table fellowship, see pp. 138–42. N.B. Here Dunn correctly points out that there were debates between the schools of Shammai and Hillel about the limits of table fellowship. That is, there was no conformity of opinion among the teachers of the Torah on this issue. If that is the case, the categorical demand of the intruders at the Antioch church for separation of the Jews from the common table indicates that they would seem to belong to the more conservative end of the spectrum of Jewish theology of dealing with Gentiles at that time.

42. 𝔭[46] and a few other manuscripts have the singular, τινα, instead of the plural, τινας, but external evidence for this variant reading is very slim. In any case, the number of the emissaries does not make a difference to the dynamic of the event here.

43. J. Louis Martyn says they are "an official delegation empowered by James" (Martyn, *Galatians*, 233). According to Gerd Lüdemann, "Both at the conference and with regard to the Antioch Christians, James was an advocate of the view that Jews must keep away from the ritually unclean tables of Gentiles, while Paul expected Jewish Christians not to abide by the Jewish dietary restrictions in their associations with Gentile Christians. The incident at Antioch must therefore be classified as an anti-Pauline action on the part of James the Lord's brother" (Lüdemann, *Opposition to Paul*, 38). Markus Bockmuehl argues that these people genuinely represented James and were not pretenders or impostors. He also says that they are not opponents of Paul and they address themselves solely to Jewish Christians (Markus Bockmuehl, "Antioch and James the Just," in *James the Just and Christian Origins*, ed. B. Chilton and C. A. Evans [Leiden: Brill, 1999], 179–182). In a technical sense Bockmuehl is right. However, the very point they address is the prohibition of the Jewish members of the Antioch church from having table fellowship with the Gentile believers. The theological basis for that point goes contrary to Paul's universalistic soteriology, in which the distinction between Jews and Gentiles is no longer meaningful. That is why Paul was so indignant about Peter's conformity with the demand of the circumcision party from James. Paul thought the fundamental truth of the gospel was at stake there. It is in that sense that I see these individuals from James as standing in continuity with other more obvious opponents of Paul in Galatians and in 2 Corinthians.

44. Murphy-O'Connor says, "The action of the delegation from Jerusalem said in effect that, though Gentile believers were 'in Christ,' they none the less remained 'sinners' because to be a Gentile and to be a sinner were one and the same thing

(Gal. 2:15b). Paul understood them to assert that the death of Christ was meaningless (Gal. 2:21b)" (Murphy-O'Connor, *Paul*, 153).

45. Lüdemann, *Opposition to Paul*, 38–39.

46. Hill, *Hellenists and Hebrews*, 142.

47. Dunn, *Jesus, Paul, and the Law*, 149–50. Here Dunn lists a number of Jewish texts that contain the word ἰουδαΐζειν. After surveying those texts, Dunn concludes that the word ἰουδαΐζειν denotes a range of possible degrees of assimilation to Jewish customs with circumcision as the end point of Judaizing. However, it is interesting to notice that in three out of the four passages cited by Dunn (LXX Esther 8:17; Theodotus in Eusebius, *Praep. ev.* 9.22.5; Josephus, *J.W.*, 2.17.10) the word ἰουδαΐζειν is used together with a reference to circumcision. According to Shaye J. D. Cohen, the term ἰουδαΐζειν has three basic meanings: (1) a political meaning, "to give political support to the Judaeans"; (2) a cultural meaning, "to adopt any of the distinctive customs and manners of the Judaeans"; (3) a linguistic meaning, "to speak the language of the Judaeans." Cohen then argues that, while the classical and Jewish usage of the term are ambiguous, Christian usage, which was heavily influenced by Paul, focuses on the religious/cultural meaning, "to adopt the customs and/or manners of the Jews" (Cohen, *The Beginnings of Jewishness*, 175–97).

48. Betz calls Gal. 2:15–21 the *propositio*, which is the thematic section of the forensic speech in Greek rhetoric, the category he applies to Galatians (Betz, *Galatians*, 113–14).

49. Brown and Meier, *Antioch and Rome*, 39.

50. The name "Antioch" appears in 2 Tim. 3:11, which is deutero-Pauline.

51. Cf. Conzelmann, *Acts*, 123.

52. The text does not even say it is the Antioch *church* that Paul visited, although that may be what is implied.

53. Dunn thinks, not unreasonably, that the Antioch Incident even influenced Paul's theology. He says, "The Antioch Incident convinced Paul that justification through faith and covenantal nomism were not two complementary emphases, but were in direct antithesis to each other. Justification through faith must determine the whole of life and not only the starting-point of discovering by God's grace" (Dunn, *Jesus, Paul, and the Law*, 162).

54. For a detailed survey of scholarly opinions on this matter, see Davies and Allison, *A Critical and Exegetical Commentary*, vol. 1, 138–47. With due caution, they also support the Antioch hypothesis as "the best educated guess."

55. For a discussion of the prominence of Peter in the Gospel of Matthew, see Davies and Allison, *A Critical and Exegetical Commentary*, vol. 2, 647–52.

56. For a reconstruction of the history of the Matthean community along this line, see Schuyler Brown, "The Matthean Community and the Gentile Mission," *NovT* 22 (1980): 193–221.

57. For Matthew's theological tendency toward universalism see Eung Chun Park, *The Mission Discourse in Matthew's Interpretation*, Wissenschaftliche Untersuchungen zum Neuen Testament 2, Reihe 81 (Tübingen: Mohr Siebeck, 1995), 167–86.

Chapter 4: Paul's Corinthian Stay and the Galatian Incident

1. There are two theories about the origin of the Galatian churches: the North Galatia Hypothesis and the South Galatia Hypothesis. The former links the foundation of the Galatian church with Acts 16:6, whereas the latter with Acts 13:14–14:26. For the history of scholarship on this issue see Bruce, *Galatians*,

3–18. Bruce himself favors the South Galatia Hypothesis and places the letter to the Galatians shortly after the Antioch Incident, which means that he regards Galatians as the first letter of Paul in the New Testament. My reconstruction of the Galatian Incident is not contingent upon the validity of either hypothesis. But, as is clear from my making connection between Gal. 4:13–14 and Acts 16:6, the North Galatia Hypothesis fits better with the course of events as I reconstruct it.

2. Betz, *Galatians*, 5.

3. Paul's expression, δι' ἀσθένειαν τῆς σαρκός (Gal. 4:13), could be a reference to an actual physical illness or it could be a metaphorical expression for difficulties of a more general kind because the word σάρξ can mean not only "flesh" or "body as physical entity" but also the earthly aspect of life in general.

4. Betz, *Galatians*, 226.

5. The phrase, διὰ πίστεως Ἰησοῦ Χριστοῦ, is doubly ambiguous. First, if Ἰησοῦ Χριστοῦ is taken to be in the objective genitive, it means "faith in Jesus Christ"; if it is in the subjective genitive, it means "faith of Jesus Christ." For a recent discussion of this problem see Paul Pollard, "The 'Faith of Christ' in Current Discussion," in *Concordia Journal* 23 (1997): 213–28. Second, the word πίστις can either mean "faith" or "faithfulness." Hence the cumbersome phrase, "the faith/faithfulness in/of Jesus Christ" in this chapter.

6. Acts does not say anything about the length of Paul's stay in Philippi. Acts 17:2 says Paul discussed the Scriptures with the Jews at the synagogue in Thessalonica for "three sabbath days," but it does not say for how much longer Paul stayed there. Lüdemann says, "Paul's stay in Thessalonica was much longer than the report presupposes" (Lüdemann, *Early Christianity*, 187). The truth of the matter is that the report in Acts does not presuppose anything about the entire length of Paul's stay in Thessalonica.

7. Lüdemann, *Early Christianity*, 184.

8. Wayne A. Meeks, *The First Urban Christians: The Social World of the Apostle Paul* (New Haven, Conn.: Yale University Press, 1983), 7–11.

9. Lüdemann, *Early Christianity*, 193, acknowledges the historicity of the Acts account of Paul's attempt at mission in Athens, although he carefully compares the differences between the Areopagus Speech and Paul's own sayings that bear similar points.

10. Cf. Thucydides, *Hist.* 1.22.

11. Suetonius, *Claud.* 25.

12. Orosius, *Historiae adversum paganos* 7.6.15–16, cited by Conzelmann, *Acts*, 151.

13. Haenchen, *Acts*, 65–66.

14. Among the seven undisputed letters of Paul, Galatians is perhaps the most difficult one to date. So there are many different conjectures. For example, Baur, *Paul*, 247–48, relying on Epiphanius's report on the order of Marcion's canon—which has the sequence of Galatians, 1–2 Corinthians, Romans—believes that it is the chronological order. Knox, *Chapters in a Life of Paul*, 71, places it "in the period of Paul's residence in Ephesus toward the end of his active career." Jewett, *A Chronology of Paul's Life*, 103, places it in the earlier period of Paul's Ephesian stay, prior to the writing of 1 Corinthians. Lüdemann, *Paul*, 99, also puts it during Paul's Ephesian period, but after the Corinthian correspondences. Bruce, *Galatians*, 55–56, thinks Galatians is the earliest letter of Paul. Betz, *Galatians*, 11–12, rightly points out the speculative nature of all the hypotheses on dating Galatians. As a working hypothesis I adopt the conjecture that Galatians was written during the late period of Paul's Corinthian stay. It allows enough time for the Galatian problem to develop after Paul's departure from Galatia and at the same time enough distance from Romans for the development of his theology between the two.

15. For the discussion of the textual problem of the phrase ἐν χάριτι Χριστοῦ in Gal. 1:6, see Metzger, *A Textual Commentary*, 520–21.
16. Betz, *Galatians*, 48.
17. J. Louis Martyn, *Galatians*, 18.
18. The text of Acts 1:21 has the noun ἀνδρῶν.
19. It is not certain whether this criterion was Luke's creation. First Corinthians 9:1 indicates that Paul's apostleship was challenged on the charge that he had not been an eyewitness of Jesus, which is an indication that Acts 1:21–22 is not entirely a redactional fiction of Luke.
20. For a recent discussion of Luke's notion of the apostles, see Andrew C. Clark, "The Role of the Apostles," in *Witness to the Gospel: The Theology of Acts*, ed. I. Howard Marshall and David Peterson (Grand Rapids: William B. Eerdmans Publishing Company, 1998), 169–90.
21. It has been noted that Galatians is the only letter of Paul that lacks a thanksgiving section, which is a conventional element in ancient Greek epistles. This omission of thanksgiving in Galatians is understandable, given the current state of relationship between Paul and the Galatian believers. However, Betz points out that the first part of the main body of the letter (1:6–11), even though it is not a traditional thanksgiving, conforms well with the Greco-Roman rhetorical convention, according to which the exordium is to be composed in such a way that it would attract the audience's attention (Betz, *Galatians*, 44–45).
22. Friedrich Blass and Albert Debrunner, *A Greek Grammar of the New Testament and Other Early Christian Literature,* tr. and rev. by Robert W. Funk (Chicago: University of Chicago Press, 1961), §1271; Herbert Weir Smyth, *Greek Grammar,* rev. ed. by G. M. Messing (Cambridge: Harvard University Press, 1956), §306(1).
23. For example, Deut. 6:25 says, "If we observe this entire commandment (אֶת־כָּל־הַמִּצְוָה הַזֹּאת) before the Lord our God, as he has commanded us, there will be righteousness for us (וּצְדָקָה תִּהְיֶה־לָּנוּ)." See also Deut. 27:26, which is a curse on the one who does not uphold the words of the Torah by observing its commandments.
24. According to Daniel Boyarin, "Moreover, it seems likely that for many Jews of the first century, not only did these practices [circumcision, kashruth, and the observances of Sabbath and the holidays] mark off the covenant community exclusively, but justification or salvation was dependent on being a member of that very community" (Daniel Boyarin, *A Radical Jew: Paul and the Politics of Identity* [Berkeley, Calif.: University of California Press, 1994], 53).
25. Witherington interprets the word μάρτυρα in Acts 1:22 as "wonderfully ambiguous" as if it could mean either an eyewitness or one who bears witness without necessarily being an eyewitness (Witherington, *Acts*, 125). But the statement in Acts 1:21–22a, taken in its entirety, clearly indicates that to have been an eyewitness was a sine qua non for an apostle. See also Clark, "The Role of the Apostles," 170–71.
26. Betz, *Galatians*, 14–23. In his analysis of the letter according to Greco-Roman rhetoric and epistolography, these sections are called *narratio* and *propositio* respectively.
27. The phrase πρὸς ὑμᾶς sounds rather awkward here because the verb διαμένειν usually takes ἐν or ἐπί with a dative. What seems to be a grammatical irregularity is due to the fact that the sentence is making an abrupt connection between the past event in the Apostolic Council in Jerusalem and the present condition of the Galatian believers. So the phrase πρὸς ὑμᾶς can be emphatically translated as "with regard to *you.*"
28. Witherington identifies the "conservative Jewish Christian faction" in Galatia with those who came to Antioch to impose circumcision on Gentile believers

(Acts 15:1) and also with those who argued for the same position in the Apostolic Council in Jerusalem (Witherington, *Acts*, 450).

29. Boyarin aptly summarizes this particular line of thought: "The doors were open, not closed, but one was saved by becoming *Jewish*. This is not, then, exclusiveness in the sense that it excludes, in principle, anyone, but neither does it conform to any Greek sense of the universal, of the One" (italics his) (Boyarin, *A Radical Jew*, 54).

30. Dunn, *Jesus, Paul, and the Law*, 220; Boyarin, *A Radical Jew*, 53.

31. For the literary composition of Galatians see Betz, *Galatians*, 16–23.

32. Boyarin says that "what motivated Paul ultimately was a profound concern for the one-ness of humanity. This concern was motivated both by certain universalistic tendencies within biblical Israelite religion and even more by the reinterpretation of these tendencies in the light of Hellenistic notions of universalism" (Boyarin, *A Radical Jew*, 52).

33. For an interesting discussion on how the letter would have been interpreted by different groups in the Galatian churches, see Martyn, *Galatians*, 27–29.

34. According to Baur, "Here (in Gal.) we first meet with those Judaising opponents with whom the Apostle had to maintain so severe a struggle in the churches which he founded." As Baur intimates here, the Galatian Incident is only the beginning of Paul's ongoing struggle with the Jewish particularists (Baur, *Paul*, 251).

Chapter 5: Paul's Ephesian Stay and the Corinthian Incident

1. The Greek text only says, ἀναβὰς καὶ ἀσπασάμενος τὴν ἐκκλησίαν.

2. It is traditionally said that this is where Paul ends his "second missionary journey" and begins his "third."

3. Cf. 1 Cor. 15:32.

4. Baur argues that Paul's opponents in 1 Corinthians are the "Cephas party" mentioned in 1 Cor. 1:12. According to his conjecture, even though Peter himself, having never visited Corinth, had nothing to do with the party under his name, the traveling "pseudo-apostles" came to Corinth and made use of his name (Baur, *Paul*, 266–67). Lüdemann sees a possible connection between the anti-Paulinism reflected in 1 Cor. 15 and Jerusalem personages (Cephas, the five hundred brethren, James) (Lüdemann, *Opposition to Paul*, 73–74).

5. It is true that 1 Cor. 8–10 deals with the issue of the idol meat, and in chap. 9 Paul uses himself as an example of the theological principle of voluntary renunciation of one's right. However, that does not necessarily mean the accusations alluded to in this section are not real. According to Richard B. Hays, "The sentence (1 Cor. 9:3) addresses not a hypothetical possibility but a situation that Paul regards as a present reality" (Richard B. Hays, *First Corinthians*, Interpretation [Louisville, Ky.: John Knox Press, 1997], 149).

6. Smyth, *Greek Grammar*, §2651.

7. Cf. Gal. 1:1, 10–12.

8. Paul's statement in 1 Cor. 7:19 reminds us of his previous saying in Gal. 5:6 and 6:15.

9. C. K. Barrett says, "It [Paul's radical un-Jewishness] rested on the conviction that in Jesus Christ Judaism had been fulfilled and the law brought to its intended goal" (C. K. Barrett, *A Commentary on the First Epistle to the Corinthians* [London: Adam & Charles Black, 1968], 211).

10. Hays, *First Corinthians*, 124.

11. For the discussion of the identity of Paul's opponents in 2 Corinthians, see Dieter Georgi, *The Opponents of Paul in Second Corinthians* (Philadelphia: Fortress Press, 1986); Lüdemann, *Opposition to Paul*, 80–97; and, more recently, Margaret E.

Thrall, *The Second Epistle to the Corinthians*, vol. 1, International Critical Commentary Series (Edinburgh: T. & T. Clark, 1994), 61–69; Jan Lambrecht, *Second Corinthians*, Sacra Pagina Series 8 (Collegeville, Minn.: Liturgical Press, 1999), 6–7.

12. Lüdemann says, "It can thus hardly be considered accidental that in 2 Cor. 11:4 'gospel' stands as the final term of the triad. In reality, it is a summary of the whole triad" (Lüdemann, *Opposition to Paul*, 92).

13. The precise translation of ἕτερον is "the other (of the two)." See Smyth, *Greek Grammar*, §1271 and Blass-Debrunner, *Greek Grammar of the New Testament*, §306(1). As such this phrase εὐαγγέλιον ἕτερον points to the gospel of the circumcision as against the gospel of the uncircumcision. See n. 22 in chap. 4.

14. Lüdemann argues that the opponents of Paul in 1–2 Corinthians are Jerusalem Jewish Christians who had been present at the Jerusalem conference and who afterward attacked Paul in his own Corinthian church (Lüdemann, *Opposition to Paul*, 94–97). I generally agree with him, but in the absence of concrete evidence of the *direct* connection between the opponents of Paul in Corinth and Jerusalem authorities, I would minimally say that the opponents of Paul in Corinth may have claimed their authority as derived from Jerusalem. Murphy-O'Connor identifies Paul's opponents in Corinth as "Judaizers" who tried to interfere with Paul's ministry in Macedonia as well (Murphy-O'Connor, *Paul*, 294–95).

15. Rudolf Bultmann, *The Second Letter to the Corinthians* (Minneapolis: Augsburg Publishing House, 1985), 177.

16. For an excellent survey of the history of scholarship on the composition of 2 Corinthians, see Hans Dieter Betz, *2 Corinthians 8 and 9: A Commentary on Two Administrative Letters of the Apostle Paul*, Hermeneia (Philadelphia: Fortress Press, 1985), 3–36.

17. The skeleton of this chronological reconstruction comes from Betz, *2 Corinthians 8 and 9*, 141–44.

18. I leave the possibility open that this section could be a part of the letter Paul mentions in 1 Cor. 5:9. For a detailed discussion of the authenticity of this passage, see Thrall, *2 Corinthians*, 25–36.

19. Murphy-O'Connor conjectures that the intruding Judaizers were aided by the "spirit-people" in the Corinthian church, who must have been offended by 1 Corinthians (Murphy-O'Connor, *Paul*, 294–95).

20. Betz, *2 Corinthians 8 and 9*, 143.

21. For the type of letter designated by the technical term ἐπιστολὴ συστατική, see C. W. Keyes, "The Greek Letter of Introduction," *American Journal of Philology* 56 (1935): 28–44. For the interpretation of 2 Cor. 3:1–3 with a textual problem and its interpretive impact, see William Baird, "Letters of Recommendation: A Study of II Cor. 3:1–3," *JBL* 80 (1961): 166–72.

22. For a discussion of their possible connection with Jerusalem, see Thrall, *2 Corinthians*, 218–19.

23. Cf. Gal. 5:1–26.

24. Cf. Boyarin, *A Radical Jew*, 7.

25. Paul often juxtaposes κατὰ σάρκα with κατὰ πνεῦμα. See Rom. 1:4; 8:4–5; and Gal. 4:29.

26. For discussions pro and contra this interpretation, see Victor Furnish, *II Corinthians*, The Anchor Bible 32A (Garden City, N.Y.: Doubleday and Co., 1984), 335; and Thrall, *2 Corinthians*, 438.

27. In the absence of any direct information, it is impossible to know who the letter carrier was. Timothy and Titus are possible candidates.

28. Baur, *Paul*, 304–307, rejects the idea of an interim visit of Paul; Bultmann, *2 Corinthians*, 45, affirms it. Furnish, *II Corinthians*, 140; Thrall, *2 Corinthians*,

164–65; and Lambrecht, *Second Corinthians*, 30–31, agree with Bultmann that there was an interim, "painful" visit of Paul prior to 2 Cor. 2:1.

29. C. K. Barrett, *A Commentary on the Second Epistle to the Corinthians* (New York: Harper & Row, 1973), 86–87 and 212–13. Based on 2 Cor. 7:11, Barrett argues that the offender in 2 Cor. 2:2 was closely associated with the Corinthian church but was not himself a Corinthian. That is, he was an intruder from outside. Murphy-O'Connor agrees with Barrett on this issue (Murphy-O'Connor, *Paul*, 293).
30. Bultmann, *2 Corinthians*, 45.
31. For a discussion on Paul's use of irony in this letter see Glenn S. Holland, "Speaking like a Fool: Irony in 2 Corinthians 10–13," in *Rhetoric and the New Testament*, ed. Stanley E. Porter and Thomas H. Olbricht, Journal for the Study of the New Testament, Supplement Series 90 (Sheffield: JSOT Press, 1993), 250–64.
32. Cf. Matt. 10:10b and Luke 10:7b.
33. The verb, παρακαλεῖσθε, is either passive or middle. I take it to be passive, meaning "be advised" or "listen to my words" rather than middle, meaning "comfort one another." See Furnish, *II Corinthians*, 582.
34. Cf. Acts 20:1.
35. Especially 2 Cor. 1:3–8.

Chapter 6: Paul's Effort for the Unity of the Church

1. James's deliberation in Acts 15:19–21 adds a list of four things that the Gentiles should abstain from (v. 20). These legal stipulations are completely missing from Paul's account of the same event in Gal. 2:1–10.
2. Romans 15:26 gives us the impression that in the end it is the churches in Macedonia and in Achaia that made substantial contributions to the collection project. However, that does not necessarily mean that other churches were not involved.
3. For arguments for 2 Cor. 8 and 9 being separate letters, see Günther Bornkamm, "The History of the Origin of the So-called Second Letter to the Corinthians," *NTS* 8 (1962): 258–64; and Betz, *2 Corinthians 8 and 9*, 3–36.
4. Bornkamm, "The History of the Origin of the So-called Second Letter to the Corinthians," 261.
5. Betz, *2 Corinthians 8 and 9*, 64–65.
6. Betz, *2 Corinthians 8 and 9*, 93–94.
7. Cf. 2 Cor. 1:15–16, which specifically mentions "to Judea."
8. With regard to Paul's wish to go to Spain, no direct reference should be made to the "great mission commandment" in Acts 1:8 or in Matt. 28:19. First of all, the authenticity of these sayings is questionable. Second, we do not know whether Paul was aware of this saying of Jesus tradition.
9. It should be noted that the word ἀπειθούντων in Rom. 15:31 does not necessarily mean "unbelievers" as the NRSV translates it. The literal meaning of the verb ἀπειθεῖν is "to disobey" or "to be disobedient." It is true that it can be used as a synonym of ἀπιστεύειν, but the semantic range of this word is not confined to this particular usage. In Rom. 15:31 it can very well mean "those who are disobedient of the new way of God's salvation of all human beings through faith in Jesus Christ not by the works of the Torah." In that sense it may include not only nonbelieving Jews but also those Jewish Christians who still object to the Torah-free gospel of Paul.
10. Cf. Jacob Jervell, "The Letter to Jerusalem," in *The Romans Debate*, revised and expanded edition, ed. Karl P. Donfried (Edinburgh: T. and T. Clark, 1991), 56. Here, Jervell argues that the essential and primary content of Romans is about the defense that Paul plans to give before the church in Jerusalem. He calls it "the collection speech."

11. According to Jacob Jervell, "In Galatians Christ is the end of the law and there-fore Israel's termination; in Romans Paul argues that Christ as 'the end of the law' does not mean the termination of Israel. With regard to sin, judgment, and right-eousness there is no difference between Jew and Greek. And yet, there is the one substantial difference, viz., that the entire non-believing Israel will find salvation because they are God's people. These are the issues he wishes to explain in Jerusalem." Jervell, "The Letter to Jerusalem," 60.

12. What stands out in that account is Paul's farewell speech to the elders of the Eph-esian church in Acts 20:18b–35. Thucydides' principle of reconstructing "what must have been most appropriate to say" (τὰ δέοντα μάλιστ' εἰπεῖν) as well as capturing the "general sense of what was actually said" (ἐγγύτατα τῆς ξυμπάσης γνώμης τῶν ἀληθῶς λεχθέντων) may apply here. In this speech the Lukan Paul talks about the danger that awaits him in Jerusalem (Acts 20:23), which is similar to Rom. 15:30–32, but it does not indicate why he is going to Jerusalem or what kind of danger he is expecting.

13. Lüdemann conjectures that Luke intentionally eliminated all the references to the collection from his source for Acts 21, because the source reported that the collection was refused by the Jerusalem church (Lüdemann, *Opposition to Paul*, 60–61).

14. Lüdemann, *Opposition to Paul*, 61: "It thus appears from an analysis of Acts 21, especially with a view to the organization and delivery of the collection, that at the time of Paul's last trip to Jerusalem the church there stood completely within Judaism and had tolerated no abrogation of the law."

15. Bruce Chilton and Craig A. Evans, eds., *James the Just and Christian Origins* (Lei-den: E. J. Brill, 1999), 5–6.

16. Stendahl, *Final Account*, presents a new interpretation of Rom. 9–11 as the heart of Romans, in which Paul acknowledges God's prerogative to save God's people Israel in their own terms, that is, without necessarily converting to Christianity. He correctly observes that in these chapters Paul self-consciously switches from his usual christocentric language to a theocentric language in order to avoid Christian exclusivism.

17. This is a good example that shows us how Paul uses the word ἀπόστολος. The context indicates that in this verse Paul simply means by ἀπόστολον "one sent (by someone)" in the etymological sense of the word. That is, there is no conno-tation of an exclusive, permanent and authoritative title in Paul's use of this word. Most probably, that is what he means when he calls himself an ἀπόστολος. The mission is a special one, but there is no need for exclusive claim for the title.

18. There is much debate among scholars on whether Paul's theology changed sig-nificantly since his conversion. To me, there is no simple answer to this question. It will depend on what one means by "theology" or by "significantly." No serious thinker remains the same with regard to his/her understanding of the self, oth-ers, and the realities, which never remain the same over the course of time. I regard Paul as one of the serious thinkers of Second Temple Judaism and early Christianity, so it is natural for me to expect from him that some of his views remained largely unaltered while other ideas of his changed in accordance with the life experiences that he went through. On this particular issue of Paul's view on the soteriological horizon, I discern a noticeable expansion of the scope toward a more inclusive notion of God's salvation, and that is what I mean by "change of Paul's theology."

19. This observation does not necessarily run counter to Martin Hengel's position in Martin Hengel and Anna Maria Schwemer, *Paul between Damascus and Antioch: The Unknown Years* (Louisville, Ky.: Westminster John Knox Press, 1997). Here, contra the view that Paul did not develop "essential" elements of his theological

view until a late phase, i.e., the time of Galatians, Hengel argues that he established his "essential" theology such as justification by faith alone without the
works of the law during the earlier, formative period between his conversion and
his "first missionary journey." I would agree with him that such a theological
understanding had already been firmly established in Paul's mind long before
Galatians was written. My interest is what happened to Paul's mind *after* Galatians. In my observation, the language of some parts of Romans and Philippians
reveals that, even though the fundamentals of his theology of salvation *sola gratia et sola fide* may have remained the same, his idea of who will ultimately be
included in God's salvation did change. He himself may have had trouble artic-
ulating his new idea clearly and that is probably why he does not make doctrinal
arguments for it. Nevertheless he shows enough of it through the language of
hope and faith in the mystery of God (Rom. 11:34–36) and the ethos of embrac-
ing others (Phil. 15–18) in his very last writings.

Chapter 7: The Aftermath

1. For discussions of what the charge might have been, see Richard Bauckham, "For
   What Offence Was James Put to Death?" and Craig A. Evans, "Jesus and James:
   Martyrs of the Temple," in Chilton and Evans, eds., *James the Just and Christian
   Origins*, 199–232 and 233–249.
2. Bauckham, "For What Offence Was James Put to Death?" 222.
3. Earlier in *Hist. eccl.* 2.1.5., Eusebius quotes a passage from Clement of Alexan-
   dria's *Hypotyposes*, which has a shorter account of the death of James. *Second
   Apocalypse of James* from the Nag Hammadi Library also contains a similar
   account. Concerning the possible relations among these texts, see F. Stanley
   Jones, "The Martyrdom of James in Hegesippus, Clement of Alexandria, and
   Christian Apocrypha, including Nag Hammadi: A Study of the Textual Relations," in *Society of Biblical Literature 1990 Seminar Papers*, ed. David Lull
   (Atlanta: Scholars Press, 1990), 322–35. See also John Painter, *Just James: The
   Brother of Jesus in History and Tradition* (Minneapolis: Fortress Press, 1999),
   113–32.
4. Eusebius, *Hist. eccl.* 2.23.1: "When Paul appealed to Caesar and was sent over to
   Rome by Festus the Jews were disappointed of the hope in which they had laid
   their plot against him and turned against James, the brother of the Lord, to whom
   the throne of the bishopric in Jerusalem had been allotted by the Apostles"
   (quoted from K. Lake's translation in the Loeb edition).
5. For discussions on this issue see Sidney Sawers, "The Circumstances and Recollection of the Pella Flight," in *Theologische Zeitschrift* 26 (1970): 305–20; and
   John J. Gunther, "The Fate of the Jerusalem Church: The Flight to Pella," in
   Theologische Zeitschrift 29 (1973): 81–94.
6. For the critical edition of the Greek text of *Homilies,* see Bernhard Rehm, ed., *Die
   Pseudoklementinen I: Homilien*, ed. Georg Strecker, 3rd ed. (Berlin: Akademie-
   Verlag, 1992); and for the Latin text of *Recognitions,* idem, *Die Pseudoklementi-
   nen II: Rekognitionen in Rufins Übersetzung*, ed. Georg Strecker, 2nd ed. (Berlin:
   Akademie-Verlag, 1994). See also F. S. Jones, *An Ancient Jewish Christian Source
   on the History of Christianity: Pseudo-Clementine Recognitions 1.27–71* (Atlanta:
   Scholars Press, 1995), 1–2.
7. For detailed discussion on anti-Paulinism in the *Pseudo-Clementines*, see Lüdemann, *Opposition to Paul in Jewish Christianity*, 169–194. Especially, concerning
   Pseudo-Clementine Homilies, Lüdemann says on p. 188, "The critique of Paul can
   be summarized as follows: Paul lacks legitimation, since he was not instructed by

the historical Jesus; his claim that Jesus had appeared to him, in view of the lack of confirming legitimation, is worthless. . . . His vision made him not into a friend of Jesus but into his enemy."

Chapter 8: Conclusions and Hermeneutical Ramifications

1. Thus, Paul's universalism, which is well articulated in Gal. 3:28, is a natural corollary to his theology of salvation *sola fide/sola gratia*, which is presented in Gal. 2:16. For Paul, *gratia*-soteriology engendered universalism, not the other way round. Boyarin takes Gal. 3:26–29 as the hermeneutical key to the entire letter. He believes that Paul was directly influenced by the Hellenistic idea of universal man and his Torah-free soteriology was a corollary to it (Boyarin, *A Radical Jew*, 23). This relation between *gratia*-based soteriology and universalism is more explicitly stated in Rom. 3:21–24 and 28–29.

2. Stendahl correctly observes that Rom. 11:33–36 is "the only doxology Paul ever wrote in God-language, without any mention of Christ or Jesus" (Stendahl, *Paul among Jews and Gentiles,* 7). I agree with Stendahl that Paul's use of theocentric language in this doxology and in the entire section, Rom. 9–11, may very well have been intentional (p. 38).

Selected Bibliography

Books

Barrett, C. K. *The Acts of the Apostles*. 2 vols. Edinburgh: T. & T. Clark, 1994.
————. *A Commentary on the First Epistle to the Corinthians*. London: Adam & Charles Black, 1968.
————. *A Commentary on the Second Epistle to the Corinthians*. New York: Harper & Row, 1973.
Baur, F. C. *Paul the Apostle of Jesus Christ, His Life and Work, His Epistles and His Doctrine: A Contribution to a Critical History of Primitive Christianity*, 2nd ed., translated by E. Zeller. London: Williams and Norgate, 1876.
Becker, Jürgen. *Paul: Apostle to the Gentiles*. Louisville, Ky.: Westminster John Knox Press, 1993.
Betz, Hans Dieter. *Galatians: A Commentary on Paul's Letter to the Churches in Galatia*. Hermeneia. Philadelphia: Fortress Press, 1979.
————. *2 Corinthians 8 and 9: A Commentary on Two Administrative Letters of the Apostle Paul*. Hermeneia. Philadelphia: Fortress Press, 1985.
The Bible and Culture Collective. *The Postmodern Bible*. New Haven, Conn.: Yale University Press, 1995.
Boyarin, Daniel. *A Radical Jew: Paul and the Politics of Identity*. Berkeley, Calif.: University of California Press, 1994.
Brown, Raymond, and John Meier. *Antioch and Rome: New Testament Cradles of Catholic Christianity*. London: Geoffrey Chapman, 1983.
Bruce, F. F. *The Epistle of Paul to the Galatians: A Commentary on the Greek Text*. Exeter: Paternoster Press, 1982.
Bultmann, Rudolf. *Theology of the New Testament*. New York: Charles Scribner's Sons, 1951.
————. *The Second Letter to the Corinthians*. Minneapolis: Augsburg Publishing House, 1985.
Buxbaum, Yitzhak. *The Life and Teaching of Hillel*. Northvale, N.J.: Jason Aronson, Inc., 1994.
Chilton, Bruce, and Craig A. Evans, eds. *James the Just and Christian Origins*. Leiden: E. J. Brill, 1999.
Cohen, Shaye J. D. *The Beginnings of Jewishness: Boundaries, Varieties, Uncertainties*. Berkeley, Calif.: University of California Press, 1999.

Conzelmann, Hans. *A Commentary on the Acts of the Apostles*. Hermeneia. Philadelphia: Fortress Press, 1987.

Davies, W. D., and D. C. Allison. *A Critical and Exegetical Commentary on the Gospel of Saint Matthew*. Vol. 3. Edinburgh: T. & T. Clark, 1997.

D'Costa, Gavin, ed. *Christian Uniqueness Reconsidered: The Myth of a Pluralistic Theology of Religions*. Maryknoll, N.Y.: Orbis Books, 1990.

Donfried, Karl P., ed. *The Romans Debate*. Revised and expanded edition. Edinburgh: T. & T. Clark, 1991.

Dunn, James D. *The Acts of the Apostles*. London: Epworth Press, 1996.

————. *Jesus, Paul, and the Law: Studies in Mark and Galatians*. Louisville, Ky.: Westminster John Knox, 1990.

————. *The Partings of the Ways: Between Christianity and Judaism and their Significance for the Character of Christianity*. London: SCM, 1991.

————. *The Theology of Paul the Apostle*. Grand Rapids: William B. Eerdmans, 1998.

Epstein, I., ed. *Hebrew-English Edition of the Babylonian Talmud: Baba Bathra*. 2 vols. London: Soncino Press, 1976.

————, ed. *Hebrew-English Edition of the Babylonian Talmud: Shabbath*. 2 vols. London: Soncino Press, 1972.

————, ed. *Hebrew-English Edition of the Babylonian Talmud: Baba Mezia*. London: Soncino Press, 1971.

Fiorenza, Elisabeth Schüssler. *In Memory of Her: A Feminist Theological Reconstruction of Christian Origins*. 10th anniversary ed. New York: Crossroad, 1994.

Funk, Robert, et al., eds. *The Five Gospels: The Search for the Authentic Words of Jesus*. New York: Polebridge Press, 1993.

Furnish, Victor. *II Corinthians*. Anchor Bible 32A. Garden City, N.Y.: Doubleday and Co., 1984.

Gager, John G. *Reinventing Paul*. New York: Oxford University Press, 2000.

Georgi, Dieter. *The Opponents of Paul in Second Corinthians*. Philadelphia: Fortress Press, 1986.

————. *Remembering the Poor: The History of Paul's Collection for Jerusalem*. Nashville: Abingdon Press, 1992.

Goodman, Martin. *Mission and Conversion: Proselytizing in the Religious History of the Roman Empire*. Oxford: Clarendon Press, 1994.

Goulder, Michael. *St. Paul versus St. Peter: A Tale of Two Missions*. Louisville, Ky.: Westminster John Knox Press, 1994.

Grant-Henderson, Anna L. *Inclusive Voices in Post-Exilic Judah*. Collegeville, Minn.: Liturgical Press, 2002.

Haenchen, Ernst. *The Acts of the Apostles: A Commentary*. Oxford: Basil Blackwell, 1971.

Hagner, Donald A., ed. *Conflicts and Challenges in Early Christianity*. Harrisburg, Pa.: Trinity Press International, 1999.

Hays, Richard B. *The Faith of Jesus Christ: The Narrative Substructure of Galatians 3:1–4:11*. 2nd ed. Grand Rapids: William B. Eerdmans, 2002.

————. *First Corinthians*. Interpretation. Louisville, Ky.: John Knox Press, 1997.

Hengel, Martin. *Acts and the History of Earliest Christianity*. London: SCM, 1979.

Hengel, Martin, and Anna Maria Schwemer. *Paul Between Damascus and Antioch: The Unknown Years*. Translated by J. Bowden. Louisville, Ky.: Westminster John Knox Press, 1997.

Hick, John, and Paul Knitter, eds. *The Myth of Christian Uniqueness: Toward a Pluralistic Theology of Religions*. Maryknoll, N.Y.: Orbis Books, 1987.

Hill, Craig C. *Hellenists and Hebrews: Reappraising Division within the Earliest Church*. Minneapolis: Fortress Press, 1992.

Jewett, Robert. *A Chronology of Paul's Life*. Philadelphia: Fortress Press, 1979.

Johnson, Sherman E. *Paul the Apostle and His Cities*. Wilmington, Del.: Michael Glazier, Inc., 1987.

Jones, F. Stanley. *An Ancient Jewish Christian Source on the History of Christianity: Pseudo-Clementine Recognitions 1.27–71*. Atlanta: Scholars Press, 1995.

Knox, John. *Chapters in a Life of Paul*. Revised and edited by D. R. A. Hare. Macon, Ga.: Mercer University Press, 1987.

Lambrecht, Jan. *Second Corinthians*. Sacra Pagina Series 8. Collegeville, Minn.: Liturgical Press, 1999.

Lüdemann, Gerd. *Early Christianity according to the Traditions in Acts*. London: SCM, 1989.

———. *Opposition to Paul in Jewish Christianity*. Minneapolis: Fortress Press, 1989.

———. *Paul: Apostle to the Gentiles: Studies in Chronology*. London: SCM, 1984.

Marshall, I. Howard. *Luke: Historian and Theologian*. London: Paternoster Press, 1970.

———. *The Acts of the Apostles*. Downers Grove, Ill.: InterVarsity Press, 1980.

Martyn, J. Louis. *Galatians: A New Translation with Introduction and Commentary*. Anchor Bible 33A. New York: Doubleday, 1997.

McKnight, Scot. *A Light among the Gentiles: Jewish Missionary Activity in the Second Temple Period*. Minneapolis: Fortress Press, 1991.

Meeks, Wayne, and Robert Wilken. *Jews and Christians in Antioch in the First Four Centuries of the Common Era*. SBL Sources for Biblical Study 13. Missoula, Mont.: Scholars Press, 1978.

Metzger, Bruce M. *A Textual Commentary on the Greek New Testament*. 2nd ed. Stuttgart: Deutsche Bibelgesellschaft, 1994.

Murphy-O'Connor, Jerome. *Paul: A Critical Life*. Oxford: Clarendon Press, 1996.

———. *St. Paul's Corinth: Text and Archaeology*. Collegeville, Minn.: The Liturgical Press, 1983.

Nadich, Judah. *The Legends of the Rabbis*. 2 vols. London: Jason Aronson, 1983.

Neusner, Jacob. *The Rabbinic Traditions about the Pharisees before 70, Part I: The Masters*. Leiden: E. J. Brill, 1971.

———, ed. *The Tosefta Translated from the Hebrew*. 6 vols. New York: KTAV Publishing House, 1977–1986.

Painter, John. *Just James: The Brother of Jesus in History and Tradition*. Minneapolis: Fortress Press, 1999.

Park, Eung Chun. *The Mission Discourse in Matthew's Interpretation*. Wissenschaftliche Untersuchungen zum Neuen Testament 2, Reihe 81. Tübingen: J. C. B. Mohr (Paul Siebeck), 1995.

Räisänen, Heikki. *Marcion, Muhammad, and the Mahatma: Exegetical Perspectives on the Encounter of Cultures and Faiths*. London: SCM Press, 1997.

Rehm, Bernhard, ed. *Die Pseudoklementinen I: Homilien*. Ed. Georg Strecker. 3rd ed. Berlin: Akademie-Verlag, 1992.

———, ed. *Die Pseudoklementinen II: Rekognitionen in Rufins Übersetzung*. Ed. Georg Strecker. 2d ed. Berlin: Akademie-Verlag, 1994.

Riesner, Rainer. *Paul's Early Period: Chronology, Mission Strategy, Theology*. Grand Rapids: Eerdmans, 1998.

Sanders, E. P. *Paul and Palestinian Judaism: A Comparison of Patterns of Religion*. Minneapolis: Fortress Press, 1977.

Schoeps, H. J. *Paul: The Theology of the Apostle in the Light of Jewish Religious History*. Translated by H. Knight. London: Lutterworth Press, 1961.

Segal, Alan F. *Paul the Convert: The Apostolate and Apostasy of Saul the Pharisee*. New Haven, Conn.: Yale University Press, 1990.

Stendahl, Krister. *Paul among Jews and Gentiles*. Philadelphia: Fortress Press, 1976.

———. *Final Account: Paul's Letter to the Romans*. Minneapolis: Fortress Press, 1995.

Tarn, William W. *Alexander the Great*. 2 vols. Cambridge: Cambridge University Press, 1948.

Thrall, Margaret E. *The Second Epistle to the Corinthians*. Vol. 1. International Critical Commentary Series. Edinburgh: T. & T. Clark, 1994.

Walters, James C. *Ethnic Issues in Paul's Letter to the Romans*. Valley Forge, Penn.: Trinity Press International, 1993.

Witherington, Ben, III. *The Acts of the Apostles: A Socio-Rhetorical Commentary*. Grand Rapids: William B. Eerdmans Publishing Company, 1998.

Articles

Badian, E. "Alexander the Great and the Unity of Mankind." *Historia: Zeitschrift für alte Geschichte* 7 (1958): 425–44.

Baird, William. "Letters of Recommendation: A Study of II Cor 3:1–3." *JBL* 80 (1961): 166–72.

Baur, F. C. "Die Christuspartei in der korinthischen Gemeinde, der Gegensatz des petrinischen und paulinischen Christentums in der alten Kirche, der Apostel Petrus in Rom." *Tübinger Zeitschrift für Theologie* (1831): 61–206.

Bockmuehl, Markus. "Antioch and James the Just." In *James the Just and Christian Origins*, edited by B. Chilton and C. A. Evans, 155–98. Leiden: E. J. Brill, 1999.

Bornkamm, Günther. "The History of the Origin of the So-called Second Letter to the Corinthians." *NTS* 8 (1962): 258–64.

Clark, Andrew C. "The Role of the Apostles." In *Witness to the Gospel: The Theology of Acts*, edited by I. Howard Marshall and David Peterson, 169–90. Grand Rapids: William B. Eerdmans Publishing Company, 1998.

Gunther, John J. "The Fate of the Jerusalem Church: The Flight to Pella." *Theologische Zeitschrift* 29 (1973): 81–94.

Holland, Glenn. "Speaking Like a Fool: Irony in 2 Corinthians 10–13." In *Rhetoric and the New Testament*, edited by Stanley Porter and Thomas Olbricht, 250–64. JSNT Series 90. Sheffield: Sheffield Academic Press, 1993.

Jervell, Jacob. "The Letter to Jerusalem." In *The Romans Debate*, revised and expanded by Karl P. Donfried. Edinburgh: T. and T. Clark, 1991.

Jones, F. Stanley. "The Martyrdom of James in Hegesippus, Clement of Alexandria, and Christian Apocrypha, including Nag Hammadi: A Study of the Textual Relations." In *Society of Biblical Literature 1990 Seminar Papers*, edited by David Lull, 322–35. Atlanta: Scholars Press, 1990.

Keyes, C. W. "The Greek Letter of Introduction." *American Journal of Philology* 56 (1935): 28–44.

Levenson, Jon D. "The Universal Horizon of Biblical Particularism." In *Ethnicity and the Bible*. Biblical Interpretation Series 19, edited by Mark G. Brett, 143–69. Leiden: E. J. Brill, 1996.

Orlinsky, Harry M. "Nationalism-Universalism and Internationalism in Ancient Israel." In *Translating and Understanding the Old Testament: Essays in Honor of Herbert Gordon May*, edited by H. T. Frank and W. L. Reed, 206–36. Nashville: Abingdon Press, 1970.

Sawers, Sidney. "The Circumstances and Recollection of the Pella Flight." *Theologische Zeitschrift* 26 (1970): 305–20.

Sawyer, John F. A. "'Blessed Be My People Egypt' (Isaiah 19.25): The Context and Meaning of a Remarkable Passage." In *A Word in Season: Essays in Honour of William McKane*. JSOT Supplement Series 42, edited by James D. Martin and Philip R. Davies, 57–71. Sheffield: JSOT Press, 1986.

Index of References

Index of Modern Authors

Index of Subjects